Considered the "Jewish Byron" by many, Peretz Markish (1895–1952) was born in Volhynia, Ukraine, and went on to write forty works in Yiddish, twenty of which were translated into Russian. In 1921, in Warsaw, he formed the group called The Gang, which struggled against realism in literature, and he coedited the expressionist *Khaliastre Almanakh,* which contained illustrations by Marc Chagall. His own poems expressed Jewish sorrow and hope. In 1926 he returned to the Soviet Union where he produced his best-known works, including those expressing Soviet patriotism and his grief at the extermination of the Jews. He was awarded the Order of Lenin in 1939, and executed in 1952, accused of Jewish nationalism.

OTHER BOOKS BY
The Dora Teitelboim Center for Yiddish Culture

All My Yesterdays Were Steps, Selected Works of Dora Teitelboim
The Last Lullaby, Poetry from the Holocaust
The Four Butterflies (children's)
The Little House (children's)
The Witness Trees
The New Country: Stories from the Yiddish About Life in America
The Jewish Book of Fables, Selected Works of Eliezer Shatynbarg
The Song That Never Died, The Poetry of Mordecai Gebirtig
A Rose Blooms Again
Sereena's Secret, Searching for Home (children's)
Proletpen, America's Rebel Yiddish Poets
Songs to a Moonstruck Lady: Women in Yiddish Poetry

INHERITANCE
(YERUSHE)

PERETZ MARKISH

Translated from the Yiddish by
MARY SCHULMAN

Edited by
MARY SCHULMAN, JOAN BRAMAN and DAVID WEINTRAUB

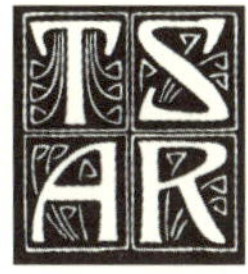

Based on the original book:
Herencia: Poemas by Peretz Markisch (*Yerushe: Lider un Poemen*)
Copyright 1959, by Editorial Icuf
Valentin Gomez 3245
Buenos Aires, Argentina

Cover designed by David Drummond

Library and Archives Canada Cataloguing in Publication

Markish, Peretz, 1895–1952.
Inheritance = Yerushe / Peretz Markish; translated by Mary Schulman; edited by Mary Schulman, Joan Braman, and David Weintraub.
-- Text in English and Yiddish.

Includes index.

ISBN 978-1-894770-42-2

I. Schulman, Mary II. Title.

PJ5129.M34Y5713 2007 839'.113 C2007-904917-6

Printed in Canada by Coach House Printing

TSAR Publications
P. O. Box 6996, Station A
Toronto, Ontario M5W 1X7
Canada

www.tsarbooks.com

TABLE OF CONTENTS

PREFACE

The Dora Teitelboim Center for Yiddish Culture, the series editor that includes this volume, is proud to include this book in its highly acclaimed collection of great Yiddish classics. Peretz Markish is one of the greatest contemporary Yiddish poets whose stirring works have barely been introduced into English. This book continues the Center's legacy of over fifteen years of publishing neglected or forgotten Yiddish works into English. This volume highlights the passion and power of Markish, a member of the Kiev lyric triumvirate with David Hofstein and Leib Kvitko who attempted to establish a modern trend in Yiddish poetry.

Dora Teitelboim, the co-founder of the Center, was an internationally renowned Yiddish poet, whose fiery social motifs sang and wept joys and sorrows and above all, the love of mankind. Ms Teitelboim, the poet for whom "the wind itself speaks Yiddish", had a dream of establishing an organization that would promote Yiddish poetry and prose to a new generation of Americans by making Yiddish works more accessible to the American public, thereby cultivating a new harvest of Yiddish educators, writers, speakers and performers.

The Center continues the dream of its namesake through publishing and translating great works of Yiddish literature, as well as developing Yiddish educational programming and documentary film, among other projects.

Yiddish has, for one thousand years, been the language of the troubadour, poet, sweatshop toiler, revolutionary and dreamer. Yiddish became the vehicle of secular Jewish life to give solid footing to a people without territory of their own. Although Yiddish fell victim to an unnatural death as a result of the Holocaust, it is experiencing a renaissance not seen for many years. This book is part of a series unearthing the hidden gems of American Jewish and Yiddish literature. And through this volume, we hope to foster a rising tide of Jewish literary creativity that fuels the perpetual burning of the great beacon of Yiddishkayt.

David Weintraub
Executive Director
Dora Teitelboim Center for Yiddish Culture
www.yiddishculture.org

FOREWORD

Some Words About Peretz Markish
ELIE WIESEL

After a lecture on Talmud in Geneva, a young academic timidly approached me and asked, "I believe that perhaps you knew my father?" It was Simon Markish, eldest son of the great Jewish poet Peretz Markish.

I had just published my novel *The Testament* in which, after numerous years of thorough investigation, I tried to evoke the lives and deaths of the communist Jewish writers, novelists, and poets murdered on Stalin's order in 1952.

My principal character, Paltiel Kossover, brought together diverse elements in each of the communist Jewish writers: their passion for justice, their thirst for fraternity, their love for the poor, for the disinherited,. They intrigued me.

I could not understand. How can a real Jew—that is, someone who seeks self-definition by and through his Jewish condition—succumb to the communist faith, which, at the extreme, preaches total assimilation? How could a traditional Jewish intellectual like Der Nister, the great novelist of the Bratslaver Hassidim, adhere to a totalitarian party in which each member is possessed to sing praises of the leader as if he were a God? How could a poet as gifted as Peretz Markish defer to the fanatical law of a Stalin? How could these men of heart and intelligence, educated in the Jewish messianic tradition, assume the roles of soldiers of communism? And then there was something else I could not understand: what made Stalin slaughter them? Why this fierce hatred? I rummaged. I studied the published and unpublished documents and letters. I questioned old, inveterate communists. I wanted to know, and I wrote the novel as much to know as to make known.

Of all the writers, two fascinated me in particular: Markish and Der Nister. First of all, because I admired their talent—the romantic inspiration of one, the poetic power of the other. I hoped to know them beyond their words.

"Perhaps you knew my father?" asked Simon Markish at my lecture on Rabbi Akiba in Geneva. I looked at him for a long moment. Was he a poet as well? "No," I said, "I never knew your father." He made a gesture of surprise. "But in your book, you speak of him so well. It is as though . . ." I interrupted him: "No, I have never met Peretz Markish, but I love him very much."

In fact, Paltiel Kossover was inspired as much by Markish as by Der Nister. Not, to be sure, on the concrete level of appearances, but on a more profound—almost invisible—level of Being. Kossover drew from their source. Like them, he wanted to sing of man, and like them, he became his victim.

Of all the commentaries on The Testament, that of Peretz Markish touched me most because it meant reward and justification.

Need I explain the attraction Peretz Markish wields on me? His character and his work are part of a landscape at once familiar and foreign—that of my adolescence. In my small town of Sighet which I believed to be the center of the universe, buried deep in the Carpathians. Immersed in his poems I found there my older friends, my precursors who, before me and better than me, dared to venture in the forbidding footpaths of action and thought outside, and sometimes against, religious tradition.

I began to read him, to study him, and have never had enough. His vision of man at war, aspiring to a simple happiness, to serenity and to love, his judgment on the enemies of the Jewish people and of all humanity—those two were always the same—and on that which constitutes their ephemeral force. His warnings, his promises, his words of consolation—you cannot read them without being distressed. His voice summons you, penetrates and tears you: you will not soon forget him.

To know him better, read and reread what his widow, Esther Markish, wrote of him, and what others published, such as commentaries on his work or on Russian Jewish poetry in general, like that of Irving Howe. Memoirs, encounters, correspondence about his turbulent years before and after the Second World War . . .

Thus I discovered a vast literature reflecting every tendency; the classic conception, lyric vocation, expressionist thrust . . . The naturalism of

Bergelson, the realism of Feffer, the mysticism of Der Nister. In every corner of the Soviet Union, Jewish writers and poets, like others, sang the new hope in which the promise still seemed beautiful and pure. An excess of naivete? Possibly. And very understandable. In those times young Jews felt the need to believe in something new. For long centuries they had suffered too much—in their person or in their collective memory—not to aspire to smash all the old structures and replace them with a revolutionary system in the bosom of which all would become possible.

Take Peretz Markish, for example.

Born in Volhynia at the end of the century, he knew poverty, misery, and fear. He attended a Jewish school, studied the holy books, sang in the synagogue, awaited the coming of the Messiah, and prayed to God to protect his people in exile. Like everyone. Then came the revolution and like so many of his contemporaries, young Markish joined its ranks. Long live liberty. Long live the future. In communist terms this meant: Down with the past, down with religion. As such, one must be freed from all that recalled tradition, the holidays, the customs, and laws, the songs and dreams off the past. The rabbis, the sages, the ancient philosophers, the bards of memory and fidelity, must yield their place to the heralds of modern socialism. Like everyone, Markish is taken by the game. In his writings of this period he praises the communists and condemns all who are not of them. Like everyone, he is hard on Jewish landlords, employers, and notables, excessively hard. And yet, several years later he is nevertheless taken to task by the political watchdogs of the party who criticize him for only portraying Jews . . . And then, unlike everyone else, he refuses to bend. He defends himself and perseveres. It is as a Jew—as a Jewish poet and as a Jewish writer—that he expressed his universal aspirations.

Is this why he left the Soviet Union in the 1920s? He goes to Berlin, to Warsaw and even visits Palestine. With Uri Zvi Grinberg and Meilekh Ravitch he founds Khalastre, a review bursting with vigor, freshness, and impertinence. He imposes himself everywhere as a brilliant and spellbinding lecturer. He upsets established ideas, unsettles all that appears secure. He puts everything in question. Ilya Ehrenburg describes him as a Jewish Byron, anxious, romantic, and possessed of a beauty that makes one dream. He could stay in the West and build a career of it. What he wants, he gets. The masses acclaim him, the elite take account of the most minor of his remarks. His humor is appealing. His courage in breaking with the traditional lyricism of Jewish poetry is valued. He is carried to triumph. And nevertheless . . . he returns to the Soviet Union.

Why? A premonition of the rise of Nazism? He senses that Western Europe is collapsing, he foresees the destruction of the Jewish communities of Poland. He is too much of a poet not to be a little of a prophet as well. In Russia a sort of Jewish cultural renaissance takes place. He publishes reviews and books in Yiddish. He teaches classes and gives colloquia. Around him one finds Kvitko and Hofstein, Halkin and Feffer, and of course, on stage, dominating them all, the great, unique Shlomo Mikhoels. Ah yes, one easily understands how a Jewish poet succumbs to this attraction. One understands his wish to be among them.

And why not say it? On the surface, Markish seems to be right. The Order of Lenin is bestowed on him. Writing in Yiddish must therefore be something important. The Stalin-Hitler pact? A passing episode. For the Jews, the war against Nazi Germany is the occasion for a full mobilization of forces to participate in the national and international struggle. One must read what Markish writes on the Warsaw Ghetto, on Jewish history in general, and above all on the war against the Jews. One must read what he wrote in his own time to understand the grandeur of his soul and the profound nature of his pain.

From then on Markish is never the same. The communist in him lives in the shadow of the Jew that he is, and whose destiny he wants to fully assume to the end. He appears to be more closed, more solitary. His poetic meditations rejoin the prophetic, classic lyricism of his distant precursors. He writes a long poem on "The Man of Forty Years" and knows that his man will only see that day posthumously. He spends more time with his son Simon. He takes account of what is happening around him: his friends and companions are being arrested. Soon it will be his turn.

On the morning of January 27, 1949 they come knocking on his door. We know nothing of what happened afterwards. How did he live in prison? What did he say to his judges and torturers? What songs did he compose in his night? I would give much to find out. In fact, now and then I say to myself that if I created Paltiel Kossover, it was to share his solitude.

(Translated from the French by Mitchell Cohen, originally published in *Jewish Frontier*, August–September, 1981)

TRANSLATOR'S INTRODUCTION

Yerushe (*Inheritance*) by the Russian Yiddish writer Peretz Markish, is a collection of poems, which he had written during 1947–1948, while seeking "peace of mind and rest" in the majestic Caucasus mountains. This was a halcyon period, before his arrest in 1948 and execution in 1952 in Stalin's purge of the Jewish writers. These poems recount his idyllic experiences among the brooding mountain crests, swiftly running springs, and shadowed pine trees, in an area known for its ancient superstitions and traditional welcome to the visitor.

Yet even in these poems celebrating nature's wonders, he sang out his sense of personal and historical tragedy: his anguish at the depopulated towns of his youth, patriotism as well as vengeance, conveyed in his lines about a rusted German helmet left behind in a cave after the defeat of Germany on Russian soil. Yet not extinguished is his vision, prophetic in tone, of a rainbow of God's promise, a golden dawn of spiritual renewal that was yet to come, for all humanity. Especially in the longer poems, most notably the monumental "To a Jewish Dancer," Markish expresses his Jewish consciousness in a sense of sorrow and heartbreak at ages-old Jewish suffering, homelessness, and wandering; but his subject is always man—his humanity and inhumanity, and his connection to nature, from its grandest to its smallest manifestations.

Despite the prevailing somber, elegiac tone of these poems, Markish does not fail to demonstrate in them his great emotional range. In the shorter, more personal and lyrical poems, based on the sights and sounds of nature and everyday life—a broken-off rose, chirping crickets, a lover's teardrop, girls sunning on a riverbank, a wild ride in a broken-down jalopy—he reveals a sensibility filled with the love of beauty and a vibrant joy of living. These feelings of a more hopeful, affirmative nature are often conveyed by him through a musical motif that runs throughout the poems.

All this outpouring of feelings was expressed by Markish through an adroit use of striking images, metaphors, and similes in a linguistically and syntactically complex style that enlarged the expressive capacities of the Yiddish language. The soul-searing power of his unique talent caused him to stand out from the other members of the *Khalastre*, that group of young, innovative Jewish writers like himself, who were the originators of a modernist movement in Yiddish literature that spread through the centers of Yiddish literature in Europe and the United States.

Despite their eccentric imagery and enigmatic, code-like expressions of ideas, due to their directness and force of expression these poems are both comprehensible and moving in their impact. For all his innovativeness, Markish worked within a framework of traditional rhyme and meter. However, an unrhymed form of verse was chosen for this translation, as best suited to expressing the nuanced complexity of the poet's ideas and the rhythms and music of his verse.

The present translation was done with a patience and devotion that could only have been inspired by the poetry itself. It is about time that work of this extraordinary poet, who was revered in his time and who I believe ranks among the greatest, should be made available to an English-speaking audience. It was my aim in doing these translations to recapture the meaning and style of the poetry in a colloquial English that manages to retain the flavor and cadences of the original Yiddish. I hope that I have succeeded in approximating for the non-Yiddish-literate reader (as well as the Yiddish audience seeking an English interpretation), the marvelous experience of reading Markish in the original Yiddish.

MARY SCHULMAN

INHERITANCE
(YERUSHE)

יערושע

לידער און פּאָעמען

POUR THE WINE, THEN

Higher than the flight of birds,
Up the mountains we ascended
To the top. And called out, —
Pour the wine with open hand,
So the future will fulfill
All our wishes and desires;

Deeper than the ocean depths
In high spirits we set out
And we toasted with a song, —
Pour the wine with open hand.
So may our people's springs be full,
And nothing ever lost of them.

Faded quickly had the summer,
And too early came the autumn.
Winter soon comes striding in, —
Pour the wine with open hand
For the near ones, for the far ones, —
And for those who will supplant us;

No regrets for being hoary,
For with brio we have lived
With our people and our land, —
Pour the wine with open hand.
Let the future, for all to envy,
Honor us in memory.

How much longer are we given
To live joyfully our lives?—
Till the very sad conclusion, —
Pour, then, pour with open hand.
Lift the cup up to the stars
In honor of our last desires.

גיסט־זשע אָן

העכער פונעם פויגלס פליגל
האָבן מיר אַף בערג געשטיגן
און דערשטיגן. און דערלאַנגט, —
גיס־זשע אָן מיט ברייטער האַנט,
אַז מעקויעם זאָלן ווערן
אַלע אונדזערע באַגערן;

טיפער פון די יאַמען גרונטן
זיך געלאָזט מיר האָבן מונטער
און פאַרטרונקען מיט געזאַנג, —
גיס־זשע אָן מיט פולער האַנט
ס׳זאָל באַם פאָלק זײַן פול די קוואָלן,
און ס׳זאָל גאָרניט גיין פאַרפאַלן;

אָפּגעבליט האָט גיך דער זומער
און דער האַרבסט איז פרי געקומען.
ערגעץ שוין דער ווינטער שפּאַנט, —
גיס־זשע אָן מיט פולער האַנט
פאַר די נאָענטע, פאַר די ווײַטע, —
די וואָס וועלן אונדז פאַרבײַטן;

ס׳טוט ניט באַנג אַזוי גרײַז און גרוי זײַן,
ווײַל געלעבט מיר האָבן ברויזנד
מיטן פאָלק און מיטן לאַנד, —
גיס־זשע אָן מיט פולער האַנט.
אַז צו גוטנס ביז מעקאָנע,
זאָל די צוקונפט אונדז דערמאָנען;

וויפל נאָך איז אונדז געגעבן
זיך צו פרייען מיטן לעבן —
ביז צום טרויעריקן ראַנד, —
גיס־זשע אָן מיט ברייטער האַנט.
הייב דעם קאָס אויף ביז די שטערן
פאַר די לעצטינקע באַגערן.

TO A JEWISH DANCER[1]

(I am Man; I behold the wretched . . .
ani gobor; reah oni . . .)
Jeremiah

I

So lightning-quick—your feet move of themselves,
In your bright and bashful bridal dance,
As if sharp knives were tossing about and colliding
And tossing their blades in their sad litany.

Cavernous, your dress's folds are surging
In fascinating, billowing waves,
As if a pursuing wind were racing beside you,
And enticed you, and entranced you with its grief—

Somewhere there's a mountain, and there's an abyss, and snow,
And on the pinnacle—above the abyss—a struggle;
—Don't be cast down—I implore you, by the woes,
Of a wanderer and of an age-old wandering.

Your feet, they're hiding something by their dancing,
But in their silvery nakedness, the anguish blazes;
As if lightning darts were tossing about and colliding
And were choking on their blades in their sad litany.

2

Where do they follow you, the wind and anguish?
Where does the wanderer pursue you on such a night?
A blizzard is outside and the snow,
And every door and gate—everywhere is shut . . .

It seems to me, that even as a child you were betrothed
To the old bachelor, the wanton sorrow;
For every night he comes to visit you
And makes you drunk with his own ancient lurking.

1. The poet's metaphor for Jewish suffering in the *goles* (the diaspora), and the disruption of life by the Holocaust.

צו אַ יידישער טענצערן

אני הגבר ראה עני
ירמיהו

.1

אַזעלכע בליציקע — זיך טראָגן דייַנע פיס
אין לייַכטן קאַלט-טאַנץ אין שעמעוודיקן דייַנעם,
ווי ס'וואָלטן מעסערס זיך געוואָרפן און געגריסט
און מיט די שאַרפן זיך געוואָרפן און געטייַנעט.

געוועלבטע בושעוועז די פאַלדן פון דייַן קלייד
מיט אַ פאַרכאַפנדיקן כוואַלישן געהויער,
ווי ס'וואָלט אַ ווינט נאָך דיר געיאָגט און דיך באַגלייט,
און דיך פאַרנאַרט, און דיך פאַרקישעפט מיט זייַן טרויער

און ס'איז אַ באַרג, און ס'איז אַן אָפּגרונט, און אַ שניי,
און אויפן שפּיץ — איבערן אָפּגרונט — אַ געראַנגל;
— זאָלסט ניט אַראָפּפאַלן, — כ'באַשווער דיך מיט דעם ווי
פון נאַ-ווענאַד און פון לאַנגיאָריקן וואַנדל.

עפּעס פאַרטייַען זיי אין טאַנצן, דייַנע פיס,
נאָר אין דער זילבערנער אַנטבלויזטקייט בלענדט דער פּייַן אויף,
ווי ס'וואָלטן בליצן זיך געוואָרפן און געגריסט
און מיט די שאַרפן זיך געוואָרגן און געטייַנעט.

.2

— וווּהין באַגלייט ער דיך דער ווינט און דער פאַרוויי?
— וווּהין פאַריאָגט דער נאַ-ווענאַד אין אַזאַ נאַכט דיך?
אַ זאַווערוכע איז אינדרויסן און אַ שניי,
און טיר-און-טויער — אומעטום זייַנען פאַרשפאַרטע . . .

מיר דאַכט זיך אויס, אַז מ'האָט דיך קינדהייַט נאָך פאַרקנאַסט
מיט דעם פאַרזעסענעם און העפקערדיקן טרויער;
אַ יעדער נאַכט קומט ער צוגיין צו דיר צו-גאַסט
און ער באַטרינקט דיך מיט זייַן אוראַלטן געלויער,

You should go with him—wherever the road—or threshold,
And lead him by the hand, in a merry dance.
—Your feet, won't they move, cramped as they are from cold?
—Your feet, won't they move, writhing as if from bonfires?

The earth is scorching you, like offerings on a pyre,
And from the sky, the cold clothes you like a dress;
Your head is silently tossed back, as for the butcher's knife[2]
And your weeping, wandering feet have lost their way . . .

3

Embrace the sorrow, then, upon your threshold,
Lead him by the hand, the shamed one, as if he were blind, —
It's likely he is kin to all the world,
And yet to one and all he is a stranger.

Also for him the sun blazed in the East,
The roads hastened to greet him, —yet again.
In every land he passed through with his plough,
In every land the people reaped his sowing.

In every land he's well known to the stars,
And in hills of ash, where he was burned alive;
The rivers never will deny the tears
Of silent mothers with their children in their arms.

As from a well, drink deeply of his pain,
And dance it out everywhere, in all the streets, and homes, —
Lead him by the hand—proudly—and go on,
For the tragic journey is not yet ended . . .

4

Does the sea ever mourn for itself with its roaring?
Does the wind, in its wandering, ever need a haven?
Out of my heart the peace was wrenched away,
It flew away—like the peahen of pure gold . . .[3]

Perhaps I should have tied her to a tree,
As once we tied our goat to a sapling tree;
But didn't the goat still run away from home?
And didn't our home itself just vanish too?
A goat it was . . . such a lovable goat . . .

2. butcher knife, or *khalef,* a ceremonial slaughter-knife
3. The fabulous peahen (*pave*) of Yiddish folk song.

זאָלסט מיט אים אומגיין — ווי אַ וועג און ווי — אַ שוועל,
זאָלסט באַ דער האַנט אים פירן, טאַנצנדיק און הייַטער;
— הייבן די פיס דען זיך ניט, קאַרטשענדיק פון קעלט?
— הייבן די פיס דען זיך ניט, קאַרטשענדיק אַף שייַטערס?

איצט בריט די ערד דיך, ווי אַ שייַטער מיט איר גאָב
און פונעם הימל טוט די קעלט איצט אַף דיר אָן זיך;
ווי פאַר אַ כאַלעף שטיל פאַרוואָרפן איז דייַן קאָפּ
און דייַנע וואַנדער־פיס די ווייַנענדיקע בלאַנדזשען...

3.

נעם אים אַרום, דעם טרויער, באַ דייַן שוועל,
פיר, ווי אַ בלינדן, פאַר דער האַנט אים, דער פאַרשעמטער, —
ער קער אָן אייגענער זיך אָן דער גאַנצער וועלט
און יעדן אייגציקן באַזונדער ז'ער אַ פרעמדער.

אויך איצט פאַר אים די זון אין מיזרעך זיך צעפלאַקערט,
די וועגן אייַלן זיך באַגעגענען אים, — נייַ.
אין יעדן לאַנד איז ער אַדורכגאַן מיטן אַקער,
אין יעדן לאַנד האָט מען געשניטן זייַן פאַרזיי.

אין יעדן לאַנד וועלן דערקאָנען אים די שטערן,
און בערגלעך אַש, ווי ער האָט לעבעדיק געברענט;
עס וועלן טייַכן ניט פאַרלייקענען די טרערן
פון שטילע מאַמעס מיט די קינדער אַף די הענט

איז טרינק זיך אָן, ווי פון אַ ברונעם, מיט זייַן וויי,
טאַנץ אוים אַף פלעצער אים, אַף גאַסן און אין הייַזער, —
פיר פאַר דער האַנט — אַ שטאַלצע — אים, און גיי,
נאָך ניט געענדיקט איז די טרויעריקע רייַזע...

4.

באַקלאָגט דער יאַם זיך דען אַמאָל אין זייַן געברום?
באַדאַרף אַ ווינט דען אין זייַן בלאַנדזשעניש אַ האַפן?
אַרויסגעריסן פון מייַן האַרץ האָט זיך די רו,
אַוועקגעפלויגן, ווי די גינגאַלדענע פאַווע...

כ'וואָלט עפּשער צובינדן באַדאַרפט זי צו אַ בוים,
ווי אונדזער ציג מ'האָט צו אַ ביימל צוגעבונדן;
נאָר איז די ציג דען ניט אַנטלאָפן פון דער היים?
און איז די היים ערגעץ אַליין דען ניט פאַרשוווּנדן?

But then she got a yen for raisins and almonds . . .[4]
So when suddenly she gave a little pull, —
Could anyone restrain her with their hands?

From all of this only a song was left to me;
I search for them throughout my ceaseless roamings;
I follow them. I utter all kinds of spells
But there's no way I can call them back to me . . .

5

A spell about a goat, who went somewhere in secret—
To carve a pathway through—from land to land;
No, the goat was never bound to any tree,
For no tree had any place to be planted.

A spell about a tree that had not yet been planted,
Yet bears the burden of blossoming and growing;
They lure it. They destroy it. They tread on it,
Yet they cannot hew it down, however sharp the axe may be.

A spell about an axe that's aiming at your throat,
For there rises from it a head higher than the sun;
There you have it, my bread. There you have it, my salt.
There you have it, my home, —my beloved home restored.

A spell about a home, about a dream of home,
That I may nevermore be driven from it;
With my own body I kneaded the clay for it
And soaked the clay in the brightness of the stars . . .

6

The glow, it was extinguished everywhere,
But a glow was streaming from your bare white knees,
When you entered in your bridal gown of clouds
And when your sorrow suddenly was rent from you.

Such a rending it was—somewhere above the mountain tops
A bird is flying by, sensing pursuit:
—Where have you heard the sound of pursuing feet?
It was just the sound of my heart falling—sawed down.

At night, my door had opened by itself,
The calm stood at the threshold bearing a bundle

4. Yet another motif of Yiddish folk song.

געווען אַ ציג... אַזאַ מין צוגעלאָזטע ציג...
האָט איר פֿאַרגלוסט זיך ראַזשינקעס מיט מאַנדלען...
געטאָן עס האָט זי מיט אַמאָל ערגעץ אַ צי, —
האָט עמעץ אײַנהאַלטן געקאָנט זי אין דער האַנט דען?

פֿון אַלץ געבליבן איז מיר בלויז אַ ליד אַליין,
איך זוך זיי אַלע אין מײַן בלאָנדזשעניש אָן אויפֿהער;
איך גיי זיי נאָך. איך זאָג זיי שפּרוכן אַלערליי
און כ׳קאָן מיט גאָרנישט זיי צוריק צו זיך פֿאַררופֿן...

5.

אַ שפּרוך וועגן אַ ציג, וואָס איז אַוועק ערגעץ געהיים —
אַדורכשנײַדן אַ וועג — פֿון לאַנד צו לאַנד זיך;
נײַן, ניט געווען די ציג געבונדן צו קײַן בוים,
ווײַל ניט געהאַט קיין בוים האָט ווו זיך צו פֿאַרפֿלאַנצן...

אַ שפּרוך וועגן אַ בוים, וואָס ניט פֿאַרפֿלאַנצטערהייט,
טראַגט ער די לאַסט אָף זיך פֿון בלִיען און פֿון וואַקסן;
מע לאַקט אים. מע פֿאַרניכט אָף אים. מע גייט,
גאָר אויסהאַקן מע קאָן אים ניט, ווי שאַרף ס׳זאָל ניט די האַק זײַן.

אַ שפּרוך וועגן אַ האַק, וואָס איז פֿאַרמאַסטן אָף דײַן האַלדז,
ווײַל ס׳שטײַגט פֿון אים אַ קאָפּ די זון אַריבער;
אָט האָסטו אים, מײַן ברויט. אָט האָסטו זי, מײַן זאַלץ.
אָט האָסטו זי, מײַן היים, — מײַן אויפֿגעריכטע ליבע.

אַ שפּרוך וועגן אַ היים, וועגן אַ כאַלעם פֿון אַ היים,
ס׳זאָל מער ניט זײַן פֿון ווו געיאָגט צו ווערן;
מיט לײַב מײַנעם פֿאַר איר געקנאָטן כ׳האָב די ליים
און אָנגעזאַפּט די ליים מיט ליכטיקייט פֿון שטערן...

6.

געווען איז אויסגעלאָשן אומעטום די שײַן,
אַ שײַן געזעצט האָט פֿון די קני דײַנע די ווײַסע,
ווען ביסט אין וואָלקנדיקן קאָלע-קלייד אַרײַן
און ווען דײַן טרויער האָט געגעבן אַ צערײַס זיך.

מיט אַזאַ רים — ערגעץ אָף שפּיצן פֿון געבערג
טראָגט זיך אַ פֿויגל דורך, דערשפּירנדיק געיעגן:
— ווו האָסטו יאָגנדיקע טריט נאָך זיך דערהערט?
כ׳האָט בלויז מײַן האַרץ געטאָן אַ פֿאַל — אונטערגעזעגן.

באַנאַכט געעפֿנט האָט זיך שטיל אַליין מײַן טיר,
די רו געשטאַנען באַ דער שוועל איז מיט אַ קלומעק

And turning to me: —I've come to say good-bye to you,
I'm leaving, and I'll never come again . . .

Inside the house was quiet. And I asked it:
—What are you taking with you in that bundle?
It answered me at once, not looking at me:
It's your heart I'm taking with me on my way . . .

7

The fluttering linen of your dress has burned away
In the flaming of your knees, the naked ones;
Only your eyebrows, they cover them so bashfully,
Only your eyes, they heal them with their brightness.

—How can one weave oneself into that radiant coil?
And—how unravel the beginning from the end?
I cannot get an answer from your mouth,
I cannot cross the divide between your lips.

It seems—I hear, how somewhere rocks are uprooted,
How rivers are overflowing—every gate;
They flow together there noisily and brightly,
And hasten—so joyfully—to rejoin the sea.

—Then let them flow. Let them hurry with great tumult.
The sea itself now overflows its shores;
I cannot get an answer from your mouth,
I cannot cross the divide between your lips . . .

8

The day is later now. The view is clear again,
The crescent moon has not yet vanished from the sky;
From pressing with my lips your golden hair
My mouth is rimmed with little golden dawns.

The day was nearing, closer, ever closer, —
Is the light enough for me? Or is it too dim?
Yet my bewildered hands still are radiant
From placing them so tenderly upon your body.

The birds are circling over me so trustfully,
They're greeting me as if they were my brothers;
—I'm drunk with your breath, as if with dew,
And my songs have suddenly begun to bloom anew . . .

און זיך געווענדט: — איך געזעגן זיך מיט דיר,
איך גיי אוועק און מער וועל איך ניט קומען...

אין שטוב איז שטיל געווען. געפרעגט האָב איך בא איר:
— וואָס נעמסטו מיט אין וועג מיט זיך דעם קלומעק?
האָט זי אַ זאָג געטאָן, ניט קוקנדיק אַף מיר:
— איך האָב דײַן האַרץ אין וועג זיך מיטגענומען...

7.

ס'ברענט אַף פון קלייד דײַנעם דער פלאַטערדיקער לײַן
אונטער דעם פײַער פון די קני דײַנע די הוילע;
נאָר דײַנע ברעמען דעקן שעמעוודיק זיי אײַן,
נאָר דײַנע אויגן זיי מיט ליכטיקייט פאַרהוילן.

— ווי וועבט מען אײַן זיך אין דעם שטראַלנדיקן קנויל?
און — ווי דעם אַנהייב און דעם סאָף פונאַנדערקניפּן?
כ'קאָן זיך קיין אייצע נאָר ניט געבן מיט דײַן מויל,
כ'קאָן ניט אַריבערגיין דעם שניט פון דײַנע ליפּן.

מיר דאַכט — איך הער, ווי ערגעץ וואַלגערן זיך פעלדזן,
ווי טײַכן טראָגן זיך — אַריבער יעדער צאַם;
זיי גיסן הילכיק דאָרט צוזאַמען אַזוי העל זיך
און יאָגן — פריידיקע — זיך אָפּגעבן דעם יאַם.

— לאָזן זיי גיין. לאָזן זיי אײַלן מיט געהויל.
דער יאַם אַליין גייט איצט די גרענעצן אַריבער;
אַז כ'קאָן קיין אייצע זיך ניט געבן מיט דײַן מויל
און כ'קאָן ניט איבערגיין דעם שניט פון דײַנע ליפּן...

8.

עס איז שוין שפּעטער טאָג. דער רוים איז ווידער קלאָר,
און פונעם הימל גייט נאָך אַלץ ניט אָפּ דער מוילעד;
פון צורירן מיט ליפּן זיך צו דײַנע האָר
באַדעקט מיט גאָלד קאַאַריקס זיך מײַן מויל האָט.

דער טאָג אַלץ נעענטער און נעענטער גענענט, —
איז מיר דען וויניק ליכט? צי ס'פעלט מיר איצט דען שײַן נאָך?
נאָך ליכטיק זײַנען מײַנע בלאַנדזשענדיקע הענט
פון צולייגן זיי צאַרט צו לײַב צו דײַנעם.

עס דרייען פייגל אַרום מיר זיך מיט פאַרטרוי,
זיי גריסן אַלע זיך צו מיר, ווי מײַנע ברידער;
— באַטרונקען מיט דײַן אָטעם, ווי מיט טוי,
האָבן פונסנײַ צעבליט זיך מײַנע לידער...

On high, the crescent moon is sharpening, as for a fencing bout,
No knife could hone itself more faithfully;
You saw it all. If it's slaughtering I deserve—then slaughter!
There could not be on earth a sweeter fate than mine.

9

Whether I sowed or harvested, —who would remember?
Whether it grew, —did anyone care about it?
Yet dark shadows are coming to demand my taxes,
Unnoticed they swoop down night after night.

Like columns of thick smoke rising from a blaze—
They drive me away with their outstretched hands;
Nor do they let me escape to any place,
Nor do they let me huddle by the walls.

They occupy my heart, as in a siege,
Like usurers—they stipulate conditions:
For every single drop of joy, it somehow seems,
I must repay with pain full seven times as much.

I see, those eyes of yours, they glisten with your tears,
I see, —yet I don't haggle. I agree to it all:
They want seven times as much, let it be seven—agreed.
If only just to have one tiny drop of joy.

10

Afterwards—with a wink—they order you
To churn out a tax agreement, exactly so;
—Churn out. —My mouth recoils with such a painful spasm
And my heart is poisoned with its bitterness.

—Where then is the heart's boundary between joy and pain?
We'll pay our tax until the end, my bright one.
Our sleepless nights will never be a burden to us
And our greatest pain will never cost too dear.

The bread, when steeped in tears, is sweet.
And bright the lightning, moving in zigzags;
It seems to me, your feet are being honed by silent shadows,
It seems to me, an abyss has besieged your heart.

נאָר ס'שלײַפֿט דער מוילעד זיך אינדר'הויך, ווי פֿאַר געפּעכט,
עס קאָן קיין מעסער שוין ניט שלייפֿן זיך געטרײַ מער;
האָסט אַלץ געזען. אויב ס'קומט מיך שעכטן — שעכט.
ניטאָ קיין גורל אױף דער ערד קיין זיסערער פֿון מײַנעם.

9.

צי כ'האָב געזײַט, צי כ'האָב געשניטן, — ווער ווייסט עס דערמאָנען?
צי אויפגעגאַן עס איז, — האָט עמעץ דען געטראַכט?
נאָר ס'קומען שאָטנס שווארצע שטײַער בײַ מיר מאָנען,
זיי לאָזן אומבאַמערקט אַראָפּ זיך נאַכט נאָך נאַכט.

ווי זײַלן רויך געדיכטע פֿון אַ סרייפֿע —
זיי טרײַבן מיך מיט אויסגעשטרעקטע הענט;
נאָר ניט זיי לאָזן מיך אין ערגעץ ניט אַנטלויפֿן
און ניט זיי לאָזן מיך זיך צוטוליען צו ווענט.

ווי אין באַלאַגערונג באַזעצן זיי זיך אין מײַן הארצן,
ווי וואָכערניקעס — נעמען אוים מיט מיר אַ טנײַ:
פֿאַר יעדן טראָפּן פֿרייד, וואָס ערגעץ בלויז מיר דאַכט זיך,
זאָל איך זיי צאָלן זיבן מאָל אַזויפֿיל פּײַן.

איך זע, ווי אויגן דײַנע, טרערנדיקע בליאַסקען,
איך זע, — נאָר כ'דינג זיך ניט. איך גיי אױף אַלעם אײַן:
זיי ווילן זיבן מאָל, איז זיבן, מאַסקים.
אַבי איין טראָפּן כאָטש אַ פֿריידיקער זאָל זײַן.

10.

דער נאָכדעם — אָפּן ווונק — זיי הייסן זיך פֿאַר דיר
אַ שטײַער-טנײַ פֿאַרקריצן פּונקט אַזאַ מין;
— פֿאַרקריצט. — גיט זיך מײַן מויל אַ ווייטיקדיקן ריר
און ס'הארץ זיך לאָזט מיט ביטערקייט פֿארסאַמען.

— ווו איז אין הארץ דער ראַנד דען צווישן פֿרייד און פּײַן?
מיר וועלן אויסצאָלן, מײַן ליכטיקע, ביז לעצט דעם שטײַער.
עס וועלן אונדז די נעכט די שלאָפֿלאָזע צו לאַסט ניט זײַן
און ס'וועט דער פּײַן דער גרעסטער אונדז ניט זײַן צו טײַער.

דאָס ברויט אין טרערן אויסגעוויקט איז זיס,
און ליכטיק איז דער בליץ, וואָס טראָגט זיך אין זיגזאַגן;
מיר דוכט, אַז שאָטנס שטיל פֿאַרשלייפֿן דיר די פֿיס,
מיר דוכט, אַז אַ טעהאָם דײַן הארצן באַלאַגערט.

The freshest springs that come from the mountain crests,
With their delightful rushing, singing waters,
Also bathe the earth's deepest foundations
And singing, remind us of the lurking chasms.

11

I thank you, wind, —no matter where you're from,
I thank you, wind, —wherever you may rush to;
The day, it clothes me in a sail of thinnest silk,
Now not a moment's joy can I have without you.

The sun has spread for me a swath of purest gold
And hordes of gay processions are awaiting;
—I thank you, —every moment is so sweet,
It beckons me to journey back to my wandering youth.

—There go the sails—ready. Here comes the breeze—outstretched.
Something my heart must reveal to the whole world;
May the distances shrink before you on your way
And the vastnesses ever be at your command.

—Do not allow the rivers any weeping.
—Do not allow the willows to bend their heads.
My beloved goes, as if to the stake, alone,
And tears are covering her downcast eyes . . .

12

Do not drink to the lees the malleable wine.
Like clustering grapes, the stars above us are swaying, circling;
Ripe they are with such an alluring glow,
Today they're sure to mislead us, as do linden blossoms—the bees.

We'll follow them. We'll pursue them to the border
And cross it, without asking—where to now?
And cross it, not knowing whether something still remains
Besides your naked maidenhood, besides my naked singing . . .

Know then, —that here, —is Creation's end and also its beginning,
So out with numbers, measures, here there's no pain;
If a bed were made for us of the blades of knives,
We would not give it up for all the world.

די פרישסטע קוואַלן פֿון די שפּיצן בערג,
כּוץ זייער רוישיקן און זינגענדיקן שטראָמען
צעשווענקען זיי נאָך אויך די גרונטן פֿון דער ערד
און, זינגענדיק, דערמאָנען זיי אין לויערדיקע טעהאָמען...

.11

איך דאַנק דיר, ווינט, — פֿונוואַנען זאָלסט ניט זײַן,
איך דאַנק דיר, ווינט, — וווּהין דו זאָלסט ניט אײַלן;
ס'טוט זיך דער טאָג אָף מיר — אַ זעגל אָן פֿון דינסטן זײַד
און כ'קאָן אָן דיר אַצינד קיין ווײַלע ניט פֿאַרווײַלן.

עס האָט די זון מיר אויסגעשפּרייט אַ גינגאָלדענע זײַל
און ס'וואָרטן מענגעס סימכעדיקע צוגן;
— אַ דאַנק דיר, — ס'איז אַזוי זיס אַ יעדער ווײַל,
עס רופֿט מיך אויף אַ רײַזע אויף מײַן הײַמלאָזיקע יוגנט.

— אַהין די זעגלען — ריכט. אַהין דעם אָטעם — שטרעק.
דער גאַנצער וועלט דאַרף איצט מײַן האַרץ עפּעס פֿאַררוימען;
זאָלן די שטרעקעס אײַנלויפֿן פֿאַר דיר אין וועג
און אונטערטעניק זאָלן זײַן צו דיר די רוימען.

— דערלויב ניט מער די טײַכן קיין געוויין.
— דערלויב ניט מער די ווערבעס שטיין געבויגן.
מײַן ליבע גייט, ווי אָף אַ שייטער אויף, אַליין,
און טרערן דעקן צו אירע אַראָפּגעלאָזטע אויגן...

.12

טרינק ביזן דעק ניט אויס דעם שמידנדיקן ווײַן,
די שטערן איבער אונדז, ווי העגנלעך ווײַנטרויבן, זיך וויגן, שפּינען;
זיי זײַנען צײַטיק מיט אַזאַ פֿאַרפֿירנדיקער שײַן,
פֿאַרפֿירן וועלן זיי אונדז הײַנט, ווי ליפּע־צווײַט — די בינען.

מיר וועלן גיין נאָך זיי. מיר וועלן נאָכגיין ביזן ראַנד
און אים אַריבערגיין, ניט פֿרעגנדיק — וווּהין גאָר,
און אים אַריבערגיין, ניט וויסנדיק, צי ז'עפּעס נאָך פֿאַראַן
אַכּוץ דײַן אָפּגעדעקטער מיידלשקייט און כּוץ מײַן נאַקעט זינגען...

דאָ איז עס, — ווייס, — דער סאָף און אָנהייב פֿון באַשאַף,
ס'איז אויס מיט צאָל און מאָס, קיין ווייטיק טוט ניט ווי דאָ;
ווען ס'זאָל אונדז זײַן אַ בעט פֿון מעסערס בלויז די שאַרף,
איז וואָלטן מיר זי פֿאַר דער גאַנצער ערד ניט אָפּגעגעבן ביידע.

Your knees are radiant. Your mouth, it is—a threshold
To a shining dawn of unimagined wonder;
Once our youth was opened up for us, like a world
And both of us have disappeared from it in flames . . .

13

From now on we'll seek each other—day after day,
The earth has not room enough for all our wanderings;
The road we traveled led us to this place,
Where trees are mourning and the birds are weeping.

We'll go on. The distances will not prevent us
From being together, from encountering each other,
It is the fate of stars to encounter one another
In their endless race, their lonely journeyings.

The snow will start to fall, the frosts will come
And winds will whisper secrets to the sands;
—Does a bird forget its nest when it's in flight?
—And doesn't then a stream always find its way?

No sharpened scythe needs to recall—the harvest, —
But I remember, I remember—it never leaves my mind,
How your hair falls over your body, like harp strings,
And I haven't yet sung out my heart on them.

14

The sea is coming towards me—all aglow
And spreads with sunlight a couch of gold for me;
—Is it then, because its skin is taut just like your body
That I can't forget you even for a moment?

Linked are the mountains, crowned by the dawn,
They call me to ascend to marvelous white castles;
—Is it then, because the heights are golden like your hair,
That I can't forget you even for an instant?

The wind, it locks me tightly in its arms,
And intoxicates me with the dews of dawn;
Is it then, because its breath is sweet, like yours,
That you can't, no matter for how long, leave my mind?

עס לײַכטן דײַנע קני. עס איז דײַן מויל — אַ שוועל
צום אויפגאַנג ליכטיקן פֿון אומבאַשיידטן װוּנדער;
געעפֿנט האָט די יונגשאַפֿט זיך, ווי ס׳עפֿנט זיך די וועלט
און ביידע זײַנען מיר דאָרט, ברענענדיק, פֿאַרשוווּנדן...

.13

און איצטער זוכן וועלן מיר זיך — טאָג נאָך טאָג,
די ערד אויף בלאָנדזשען זײַן אַצינדערט וועט אונדז ווייניק;
עס האָט אונדז אויף אַ וועג אַזאַ געגעבן אַ פֿאַרטראָג,
ווי ביימער טרויערן און ווי די פֿייגל וויינען.

מיר וועלן גיין. עס וועט די ווײַטקייט אונדז ניט זײַן קיין שטער
אויף זײַן באַנאַנד, אויף איינס דעם צווייטן אָנזען,
ווי אָנזען איינס דעם צווייטן איז די שטערן זיך באַשערט
אין זייער אייביקן געיעג, אין זייער איינזאַמיקן בלאָנדזשען.

אַראָפּגיין וועט אַ שניי און דורכגיין וועלן פֿרעסט
און ווינטן וועלן ווידער עפּעס אײַנרוימען די זאַמדן;
— פֿאַרגעסט אַ פֿויגל דען אין וואַנדערונג זײַן נעסט?
— און ס׳טרעפֿט אַ שטראָם דעם וועג ניט צו דעם דען?

אין שניט דערמאָנען — ניט דער שנײַדמעסער באַדאָרף, —
כ׳געדענק, כ׳געדענק, — ס׳פֿאַרשווינדט ניט פֿון מײַן זין גאָר,
אַז ס׳פֿאַלן אויף דײַן לײַב די האָר, ווי סטרונעס אויף אַ האַרף,
און איך האָב נאָך מײַן האַרץ אויף זיי ניט אויסגעזונגען.

.14

עס גייט דער יאַם אַנטקעגן מיר — צעהעלט
און בעט מיט זון פֿאַר מיר אַ גאָלדענעם געלעגער;
— צי דען דערפֿאַר, וואָס שטײַף איז, ווי דײַן לײַב, זײַן וועל
קאָן איך זיך דען פֿון דיר פֿאַרגעסן אויף אַ רעגע?

עס קײַטלען זיך געבערג, געקרוינטע מיט קאַיאָר,
זיי רופֿן מיך אינדר׳הויך, אין ווײַסע ווּנדערלעכע שלעסער;
— צי דען דערפֿאַר, וואָס זייער הויך ז׳באַגילט, ווי דײַנע האָר
קאָן איך אַפֿילע דען אַן אויגנבליק אין דיר פֿאַרגעסן?

דער ווינט גיט מיך אין זײַנע אָרעמס אַ פֿאַרשלים
און טרינקט מיך אָן מיט זאַפֿטן פֿון באַגינען;
— צי דען דערפֿאַר, וואָס ער איז, ווי דײַן אָטעם, זיס
קאָנסטו אויף וויפֿל דען ניט איז אַרוים מיר פֿונעם זינען?

I did not hone my heart at the forbidden threshold,
I don't know how to read the Stone of Wisdom, —
But say—why can I see the entire world in you
Though the world itself is not enough to replace you? . . .

15

I meet the day alone, alone I follow it
And in the night no sleep comes to my eyes;
—Unwillingly, I caused you so much pain,
Punish me, dearest, more than I have suffered.

Your shadow falls from every tree, wherever one treads,
Yet the sound of their singing does not turn my head;
—I cannot ransom even with all my songs
The least one of your tears, that courses down your cheek.

Staring into space above are the burnt-out mountains,
Lightly from one to another they toss the breezes;
—How can I reach out to you these mourning hands,
Dipped as they are in your moonlit body's glow?

Every wind I meet, and every wind I follow,
Sorrowfully I gaze upon their frenzied rush;
Unwillingly I caused you so much pain,
Punish me, dearest, more than I have suffered.

16

Somewhere the herds are descending to the valleys,
The day is waning at the heads of dismal mountains;
By shepherds' pipes your voice is carried to me
And by the ocean's surf—your hidden reproach.

That flowing voice of yours—can slake the thirst of one who's thirsting,
It seems to trickle down from mountaintops to seas;
I lie in wait for them, the winds of dawn,
That I should not miss seeing them take flight.

Have no quarrel with me, you winds, —and I turned
To each and every one of them, as to a mother, —
With whom could I have sent my heart away,
As one would send a letter on some such occasion?

כ׳האָב ניט געשלײַפט מײַן האַרץ באַ דער פאַרווערטער שוועל
און כ׳ווייס ניט ווי דעם שטיין פון כאָכמע זאָל איך לייענען, —
נאָר זאָג — פאַרוואָס איז לײַכט אַזוי צו זען אין דיר די גאַנצע וועלט
און נאָר די וועלט איז ניט אומשטאַנד פאַרבײַטן דיך אַליין נאָר ? . . .

.15

דעם טאָג באַגעגן איך אַליין, אַליין דעם טאָג באַגלייט איך
און ס׳קומט באַנאַכט אַף מײַנע אויגן ניט קיין שלאָף ;
-- איך האָב דיר אומגערן פאַרשאַפט אַזויפיל ווייטאָק,
באַשטראָף מיך, טײַערע, נאָך מער, ווי כ׳בין באַשטראָפט.

דײַן שאָטן פאַלט פון יעדן בוים אַף שריט און טריט דאָ,
נאָר זייער זינגענדיקער רויש זיך ווענדט פון מיר ניט אָפ ;
— איך וועל ניט אויסקויפן מיט אַלע מײַנע לידער
די מינדסטע טרער, וואָס טריפט פון דיר אַראָפ.

פאַרקוקט אינדר׳הויך האָבן געבערג זיך אָפגעברענטע,
זיי שיקן ווינטלעך איינס צום צווייטן אַזוי לײַכט ;
— ווי שטרעקט מען אויס אַזוי די טרויעריקע הענט דיר,
וואָס זײַנען אײַנגעטונקט אין ליכט פון דײַן לעוואָנעדיקן לײַב ?

אַ יעדן ווינט באַגעגן איך, אַ יעדן ווינט באַגלייט איך,
מיט טרויער קוק איך נאָך נאָך זייער האַסטיקן געלאָף ;
— איך האָב דיר אומגערן פאַרשאַפט אַזויפיל ווייטיק,
באַשטראָפן מיך, טײַערע, נאָך מער, ווי כ׳בין באַשטראָפט.

.16

עס לאָזן ערגעץ טשערעדעס אַראָפ זיך שוין אין טאָל,
דער טאָג איז אויסגעגאַן צוקאָפנס אַף געבערג אַף טריבע ;
דורך פאַסטעכדיקע פײַפעלעך דערטראָגט זיך מיר דײַן קאָל
און דורכן צושלאָג פונעם יאַם — דײַן פאַרבאַהאַלטענער פאַראיבל.

דײַן פליסנד קאָל — אַ דאָרשטיקן קאָן אײַנשטילן דעם דאָרשט,
מע ריזלט, דאַכט זיך, אויך פון שפיצן-בערג צו יאַמען ;
איך האָב זיי אויסגעטשאַטשעוועט, די ווינטן פון קאַיאָר,
איך זאָל צו זייער ווײַטן אָפילי ניט פאַרזאַמען.

— האָט קיין פאַראיבל מיר ניט, ווינטן, — זיך געווענדט,
האָב איך צו יעדן אײנציקן פון זיי, ווי צו אַ מאַמע, —
מיט וועמען וואָלט איך עס מײַן האַרץ אַוועקשיקן געקאָנט,
אָט ווי מע שיקט אַוועק אַ בריוו מיט אַ געלעגנהײַט אַזאַ מין ?

—Here, read it, my heart—just as it is,
Reading it will surely take you all night long;
Myself, I hurried past and greeted no one,
I cannot yet compose a pretty letter . . .

17

The ripened stalk falls to the scythe alone
With throat stretched out, so golden and so desolate:
—Well, open it, look inside my heart, and read,
For I myself don't know what's written there . . .

Everything is there engraved, as with a knife.
So you must take it with you wherever you go;
It seems to me that embedded there is your own writing,
And no one else but you could read what's written there.

How can I make you understand I wonder,
So that you leave out no word, nor forget a single one?
Nor should you overlook even one letter, —
For everything is there engraved as with a knife.

From dawn to dawn I will wait here alone
With throat outstretched in my own mournful song;
—Well, open up my heart—and look, and read,
For I myself don't know what's written there . . .

18

The wedding clamor is heard in the streets again,
From the gaiety the weeping is again awakened;
Only the fiddles and the contrabasses have been smashed,
Only the musicians have been murdered on their way.

And you? —You, dance . . . placing your feet as over webs;
The heart with your own pain—deafen it.
And bear it, bear, the sorrow of the bridal seating,[5]
As for the slaughter the dove offers its soft throat.

The head—bowed down, the eyes—in chains,
The distant stars accompany them by night;
Thus had the mothers ever gone to the *akeyde*,[6]
And brought for themselves the faggots and the fire.

5. *bazetsns*: At a wedding, the bride is "seated" (*bazetst*), before she is taken under the canopy (*khupe*).
6. *akeyde:* Hebrew word for "sacrificial altar."

— נאַ, לייען עס, דאָס האַרץ — אַזוי ווי ס'איז,
ס'וועט אַף אַ נאַכט אַ גאַנצער קלעקן דיר צום לייענען;
כ'האָב זיך אַזוי געאײַלט און קיינעם ניט געגריסט,
איך קאָן נאָך אַלץ קיין בריוו ניט אויסשטעלן קיין שיינעם...

.17

די רײַפֿע זאַנג פֿאַלט אַף שנײַדמעסער אַליין
מיט אויסגעשטרעקטן האַלדז מיט גאָלדענעם און טריבן:
— נו, עפֿן עס, מײַן האַרץ און קוק, און לייען,
אַז כ'ווייס גאָרניט אַליין, וואָס דאָרטן איז געשריבן...

ס'איז דאָרטן אַלץ פֿאַרקריצט אַזוי ווי מיט אַ מעסער.
דו זאָלסט מיט דעם אינערגעץ ניט פֿאַרגיין נאָר;
מיר דאַכט, אַז דאָרטן איז צעזייט דײַן אייגן קסאַוו,
אַז לייענען, כוץ דיר, וועט עס ניט קאָנען קיינער.

ווי גיט מען צו פֿאַרשטיין דיר און מיט וואָס,
אַז זאָלסט ניט דורכלאָזן קיין וואָרט, קיין איינציקס ניט פֿאַרגעסן?
דו זאָלסט ניט איבערהיפּערן קיין אָס, —
ס'איז דאָרטן אַלץ פֿאַרקריצט אַזוי ווי מיט אַ מעסער.

כ'„וועל פֿון באַגינען ביז באַגינען וואַרטן דאָ אַליין
מיט אויסגעשטרעקטן האַלדז פֿון ליד מײַנער פֿון טריבער;
— נו, עפֿן עס, מײַן האַרץ, און — קוק, און לייען,
אַז כ'ווייס גאָרניט אַליין, וואָס דאָרטן איז געשריבן...

.18

דער ראָש פֿון כאַסענעס איז ווידער אַף די גאַסן,
פֿון סימכעס דאָס געוויין איז אָפּדאָסנײַ דערוועקט;
צעבראָכן זײַנען בלויז די פֿידלען און די קאָנטראַבאַסן,
געקוילעט זײַנען בלויז די קלעזמער אַפֿן וועג.

נאָר דו? — דו, טאַנץ.. די פֿיס געשטעלט, ווי איבער נעצן,
דאָס האַרץ מיט וויטיק אייגענעם — פֿאַרטויב.
און טראָג אים, טראָג, דעם טרויער פֿון באַזעצנס,
ווי צו דער שכיטע טראָגט דעם האַלדז די מילדע טויב.

דעם קאָפּ — אַראָפּגעלאָזט, די אויגן — אויפֿגעקייטלט,
ס'באַגלייטן ווײַטע שטערן באַ דער נאַכט;
עס זײַנען מאַמעס אָט אַזוי געגאַן צו דער אַקיידע,
דאָס פֿײַער און דאָס האָלץ אַליין פֿאַר זיך געבראַכט.

So from your body tear strips of living flesh
And—dance, the imagined distances—awaken.
Only the fiddles and the contrabasses have been smashed,
Only the musicians have been murdered on their way.

19

A noise of eagles warns of danger at the threshold
From that armored and unapproachable ancientness;
Though clever little paths, that snake among the boulders,
Have lured me, straying, to the waterfall *Agura*.[7]

The stream that rushes from the mountain crests, —
To the precipice still murmurs its complaint,
—Come nearer, homeless one, come nearer here,
It will wash the dust from your long-wandering feet.

I know not—whose defeat it is and whose the victory;
Heads pillowed upon rocks—storms are snoring in their sleep.
Also for you the rocks shall make a splendid cradle,
And you shall behold a stairway from abyss to heaven . . .

In the chaos of the cavern of the Creation,
With the eternal speech of your so weary feet, —
Tell the waterfall, tell it alone,
How for two thousand years, in chains, you strove towards mountains.

20

Tell it, my homeless one, enchant it so that it remembers, —
Right now you're dancing for a flock of mountains,
For in the world there's no one left for you;
And you have no one to turn to any more.

Uprooted, your brothers are roaming over seas,
Begrudged by the earth a haven or a shore;
No child can ever find where is its mother
And neither can a mother ever find her child.

Their eyes they put out for looking at the stars,
Their mouths they burned just for their sunlit song.
They will reach from the abyss to the unchanging stars,
Bound up in darkening clouds and dazzling light.

7. *Agura*: I could not find any reference to this word anywhere; perhaps it is a proper name.

איז רײַם פון לײַב זיך לעבעדיקע פּאַסן
און — טאַניץ, און ווײַטן דרעמלדיקן — וועק.
צעבראָכן זײַנען בלויז די פידלען און די קאָנטראַבאַסן,
געקוילעט זײַנען נאָר די קלעזמער אַפן וועג.

.19

אַן אָדלער־רויש וועגן געפאַרן האָרנט באַ דער שוועל
פון דעם פאַרפאַנצערטן, ניט־צוטריטלעכן אוראַלט;
נאָר קלוגע סטעזשקעלעך. וואָס שלענגלען זיך פון פעלדז
האָבן מיך, בלאָנדזשענדיק. פאַרפירט צום וואַסערפאַל אגורא.

דער רוישנדיקער שטראָם פון שפּיצן בערג, —
נאָך אַלץ עפּעס דעם אָפּגרונט טײַנעט דאָרט אַרײַן ער;
— גענען, מײַן הײמלאָזע, גענען אַהער,
ער וועט דיר אָפּוואַשן דעם שטויב פון בלאָנדזשענדיקע פּיס
פון דײַנע.

איך ווייס ניט — וועמעס בראָך איז דאָ און וועמעס זיג,
מיט שטיין צוקאָפּנס — שטורעמס אײַנגעשלאָפן כראָפּען;
דיר וועלן אויכעט שטיינער זײַן אַ וווּנדערלעכע וויג,
אַ לייטער וועסט דערזען צום הימל פונעם אָפּגרונט...

אין דער אומאָרדענונג פון בערײשיסדיקער הייל
מיט שפּראַך מיט אייביקער פון דײַנע פּיס די מידע, —
בלויז אים אַליין, דעם וואַסער־פאַל, דערצייל,
ווי צו די באַרג־שפּיצן צוויי טויזנט יאָר דו רײַסט זיך, אַ געשמידטע.

.20

דערצייל, מײַן הײמלאָזע, פאַרקישעף און דערמאָן אים, —
אַצינדערט טאַנצסטו פאַר אַן איידע בערג;
פאַר דיר איז קיינער אין דער וועלט דאָרט ניט פאַראַנען,
דו האָסט צו וועמען זיך ניט ווענדן מער.

פאַרשטויסן וואָגלען ברידער אום איבער די יאַמען,
קיין האַפן און קיין ברעג די ערד זיי ניט פאַרגינט;
עס קאָן קיין קינד ניט אָפּזוכן זײַן מאַמען
און ס׳קאָן קיין מאַמע מער ניט טרעפן צו איר קינד.

די אויגן אויסגעשטאָכן האָט מען זיי פאַר קוקן צו די שטערן
און פאַר דעם זוניק ליד האָט מען די מײַלער זיי געברענט,
צום אָפּגרונט ס׳וועט דערגיין און צו די שטייגעריקע שטערן,
פאַרבונדענע מיט כמאַרע און מיט בלענד.

You have no one any more. There is no solace,
Mountain and cave will choke upon your woe;
The depths will hasten to rise up to you, —
Dance, dance, my homeless one, —enchant them, tell them.

21

What more is there to do in your lonesome, driven journey?
Bid your farewell, and do it quickly, hurrying by.
You have not yet paid your tax for wanting to be free,
Yet now they command you to bring your head to them.

No grain has grown in the fields to fill us,
Yet your debt to them has increased in amount;
For wanting to think, to dream, and having dared,
You must not haggle, —pay up.

The gold—stolen, the jewels—flung about,
An empty cradle standing by the threshold;
A bonfire has been kindled and awaits you,
You'll pay with your head for the love you bear the world.

So dance it all out, before the flames consume you,
Lash the shame—from the body, the body—from the bones.
You have not paid up your tax for wanting freedom,
For the freedom to hold high your grieving head . . .

22

Tell the waterfall, each mountain can recall it,
It's carved in every mountain by the blaze of dawn—
That first echoing call from above them—"Do not kill!",
Now rolling around in ashes, covered with green mold

—Know, you mountains—that the war with darkness still goes on,
This thought won't yield one solitary step;
Not defeated is he whose sorrowing head falls to the axe,
But he, who wields the axe so lightly within his head.

—Then know, you mountains—know too, you distances,
The open road to thought keeps death at bay.
Not he the victor, who puts a bridle on another,
But he, the bridled one, who shatters it.

האָסט מער דאָרט קיינעם ניט. דאָרט איז קיין טרייסט ניטאָ מער,
ס'וועט מיט דײַן ווײ דערוואָרגן זיך דער באַרג און הייל;
באַרוישט זיך אויפהייבן צו דיר וועלן די טהאָמען, —
טאַנץ, טאַנץ, מײַן היימלאָזע, — פאַרקישעף און דערצייל.

.21

וואָס האָסטו נאָך אין דײַן געיאָגטער אומעטיקער רײַזע?
געזעגן זיך און גיב עס שנעל און אײַליק אָפּ.
האָסט נאָך ניט אויסגעצאָלט דעם צינדז פאַר וועלן פרײַ זײַן,
מע הייסט אַצינדערט ברענגען זיך דײַן קאָפּ.

קיין ברויט אין פעלד צו זאַט איז ניט געוואַקסן,
אָבער דער כויוו פון דיר געשטיגן איז אין צאָל;
פאַר וועלן דענקען, טרוימען און געוואָגט זײַן,
איז ניט געדונגען זיך, — באַצאָל.

דאָס גאָלד — אַוועקגערויבט, דאָס צירונג איז צעשלײַדערט
און ס'שטייט אַ וויגעלע אַ ליידיקס בײַ דער שוועל;
ס'איז אָנגעצונדן פאַר דיר אַ שייטער,
ביסט שולדיק מיטן קאָפּ פאַר דײַן פאַרליבטקייט אין דער וועלט.

איז טאַנץ זיך אוים איידער דער פלאַם וועט דיך צעבײַסן,
די שאַנד — פון לײַב, דאָס לײַב — פון ביינער שמײַס אַראָפּ.
האָסט נאָך ניט אויסגעצאָלט דעם צינדז פאַר וועלן פרײַ זײַן,
פאַר טראָגן פרײַ דײַן טרויעריקן קאָפּ...

.22

ד'ערצייל דעם וואַסערפאַל, דערמאָנען קאָן אַ יעדער באַרג אים,
אין יעדן באַרג איז אויסגעקריצט מיט פײַער פון באַגין —
דער דורכגעהילכטער איבער זיי צום ערשטן מאָל — „ניט הארגע!",
וואָס וואָלגערט זיך אין אַש, באַדעקט מיט שימלדיקן גרין.

— זײַט וויסן, בערג, — די קריג מיט פינצטערנישן דויערט,
קיין שפּאַן קיין איינציקן טרעט דער געדאַנק ניט אָפּ,
באַזיגט ז'ניט דער אַ וועמעס קאָפּ פאַלט פון דער האַק אין טרויער,
נאָר יענער, וואָס די האַק בלויז לײַכט בײַ אים אין קאָפּ.

— זײַט וויסן, בערג, — זאָל אײַך באַוווסט זײַן, רוימען,
דער צוטריט צום געדאַנק ז'דעם טויט פאַרווערט.
אַ זיגער איז ניט דער, וואָס טוט דעם אַנדערן אַ צוים אָן,
נאָר דער, וואָס אין דער צוים — די צוים צעברעכט.

So dance, my homeless one, as long as distances remain,
And let the roaring waterfall engulf you.
Not dead is he who is burned upon the pyre,
But he who in the flames sees only smoldering ashes.

23

He comes, he comes, the Golem with the axe,
To introduce a new order to old temples;
From his apelike shoulders a sack is dangling,
Inside a desecrated corpse, that he slew along the way.

A yellow patch is seared into the corpse,
Just chunks of flesh—torn-out pockets—stark naked;
—It's long since he has had such fatty meals,[8] —
Gorging himself, the drooling Golem licks his chops.

His blood-stained lips are moving thickly,
Dumbly beseeching his revered lord god for help and counsel;
He comes, he comes—slobbering and belching,
And a sadness falls upon him, and a horror.

The patch sticks in his throat. It won't go down.
Already there's a stridor, he's choking on it.
He'll soon be at your doorstep: —do you know some sort of spell,
To make him vomit both the patch and his own gullet?

24

By dancing, homeless one, you'll deafen it, drown it out,
May ill pursue him for ten generations;
This won't be entered into the ledger books,
Nor will any words serve as collateral.

The morning brightness rushes in with the dawn,
The winds awaken the distances with their humming.
His body will be etched with naked spears
And it will be engraved upon his skin with blood.

Every mountain, with boulders tottering, is waiting;
And sea is asking sea, from whence a flood;
Graves will rise up from Rotterdam to Warsaw,
Graves will rise up from every wiped-out road.

8. *kest*: "essn kest"—to "eat board"; a father supported a son-in-law, to enable him to study Talmud without financial worry.

איז טאַנץ, מײַן הײמלאַזע, קאַלומאַן פֿאַראַן ס'איז נאָך װײַטן,
און פֿאַלן לאָז אַף זיך פֿון װאַסערפֿאַל דעם ראַש.
ס'איז טױט ניט דער, װאָס װערט פֿאַרברענט אַף שײַטערס,
נאָר דער, װאָס זעט אין פֿלאַם בלױז טליִענדיקן אַש.

.23

ער גײט, ער גײט, דער גזילעם מיט דער האַק
איבער די אַלטע טעמפּלען אײַנפֿירן אַ נײַע אָרדענונג;
אַף זײַנע מאַלפּעדיקע אַקסלען באַמבלט זיך אַ זאַק
מיט אַ געשענדטן בארמינען, װאָס ער האָט אַפּן װעג דערמאָרדעט.

אַ געלע לאַטע אױסגעבערענט איז אַף דעם מעס,
מיט שטיקער פֿלײש — די טאַשן אױסגעריסן — הױלע;
— ער האָט פֿון לאַנג שױן ניט געהאַט אַזעלכע פֿעטע קעסט, —
באַלעקט זיך, פֿרעסנדיק אין װעג, דער גאַװערדיקער גזילעם.

די ליפּן רױדערן שװער אין בלוט פֿאַרפֿלעקט
צום ליבנסװירדיקן הער גאָט פֿאַר הילף און ראַט געהײמען;
ער גײט, ער גײט, — ער גאַזערט און ער גרעפּצט,
און ס'פֿאַלט אים אָן אָן אומעט און אָן אײמע.

די לאַטע שטעלט זיך אים אין האַלדז. זי קריכט ניט דורך.
ער כריפּעט שױן. ער װערט פֿון איר דערװאָרגן,
ער װעט נאָך קומען צו דײַן שװעל: — צי װײסטו ניט אַזאַ
מין שפּרוך,
די לאַטע אױסברעכן זאָל ער אינײנעם מיטן גאָרגל?

.24

מיט טענץ, מײַן הײמלאָזע, פֿאַרטױב עס און פֿאַרטרינק עס,
זאָל אים דער בראָך פֿאַרפֿאַלגן ביזן צענטן דאָר;
פֿאַרשריבן װערן מער ניט זײַן ס'װעט אין קײן פּינקעס
און אײַנלײגן ניט קאָנען ס'װעט זיך אין קײן װאָרט.

עס אײַלט שױן מיט באַגין דער העלער אינדערפֿרי זיך
און װינטן װעקן אױף די װײַט מיט אַ געהױד;
ס'װעט אַף זײַן לײַב זיך אױסקריצן מיט בלױזע שפּיזן
און אַף זײַן הױט פֿאַרשריבן װערן ס'װעט מיט בלוט.

אַ יעדער באַרג מיט שטײנער אױפֿגעװיגטע װאָרט שױן
און יאַם באַ יאַם אַף אַ פֿאַרפּלײצונג פֿרעגט;
ס'װעלן זיך קװאָרים אױפֿהײבן פֿון ראָטערדאַם ביז װאַרשע,
ס'װעלן זיך קװאָרים אױפֿהײבן פֿון יעדן אָפּגעמעקטן װעג.

No one will then be able to keep records
Of every pain and tragedy that took place;
—Let the pain not vanish with the echo of your dancing,
For we need to read it in your wandering feet.

25

—So beat it out, that scorching madrigal,
Your dancing feet shall nothing disavow.
The Golem's yellow gall is burning on you—
That which, —drunk with blood, —he vomited up.

Thank him, homeless one, thank him for his gift,
For nothing else had he in his possession;
You paid him with your gray head for a night's lodging,
And upon you he fastened a yellow patch.

What else does he think you owe him for the lodging?
Right from the start he robbed you of your bundle.
The bread from your sack—devoured—finished,
As if it never was and now—all gone.

So—quits.
Good-bye. For surely his mouth is shut forever.
So what's the reason he's still counting your steps?
What more does the Golem want from you?

26

The heart? The brain? Like a snake, into their deepest depths,
He gnawed them, then vomited them up, like undigested food;
The only thing the snake holds dear is his poison,
The rest of him is doomed to crawl upon the earth.

He will not rise above the grass on the graves,
Beneath it—his victories are ever on the increase;
He'll come there with his sword to bang out the rust
And feed in the darkness together with the worms.

And then compare himself with them in girth,
And in his rank, his greed, and in loathesomeness;
It doesn't matter—that he placed a patch upon you,
Instead of covering with it his own shame.

קיין פינקעס אויפשטעלן וועט קיינער ניט אומשטאַנד זײַן
מיט יענעם פײַן און טרויער, ווי געוועזן עס איז ;
— זאָל ניט פאַרגיין דער ווײי אין אָפּהילך פון דײַן טאַנצן,
מע דאַרף עס אויסלייענען אין דײַנע וואַנדעראָוונע פּיס.

.25

— נו, קלאַפּ אים אויס, דעם הייסן מאַדריגאַל,
דורך דײַנע פּיס זאָל גאַרניט זײַן פאַרלייקנט.
זי ברענט אַף דיר, דעם גוילעמס גנעלע גאַל,
וואָס ער — פון בלוט אַ שיקערער — האָט אויסגעמייִקעט.

באַדאַנק אים, היימלאָזע, באַדאַנק אים פאַר דער גאָב,
ער האָט דאָך מער אַף זײַן פאַרמעגן ניט געהאַט דאָך ;
דו האָסט פאַר נאַכטלעגע אים באַצאָלט דײַן גרײַזן קאָפּ
און ער האָט צוגעדעקט דיך מיט אַ געלער לאַטע.

וואָס קומט אים נאָך אַרויס צום כעשבן פאַר דעם נאַכטלעג ?
דעם קלומעק — צוגערויבט האָט ער נאָך פון פאַרויס.
דאָס ברויט פון טאַרבע — אויפגעפרעסן — פאַרטיק,
ווי ניט געוועזן און -- אויס.

און — קוויט.
אַ גוטן טאָג. פאַרשטאָפּט ביז לעצט דאָס מויל אים.
איז וואָס-זשע ציילט ער ווײַטער דײַנע טריט ?
וואָס נאָך פאַרלאַנגט פון דיר דער גוילעם ?

.26

דאָס האַרץ ? דעם מאַרך ? ער, ווי אַ שלאַנג האָט ביז דער טיפסטער טיף
זיי אויסגענאָגט און אויסגעבראָכן צוריק, ווי ניט-פאַרדײַעטע געקעכצן ;
דאָס איינציקע, וואָס טראָגט דער שלאַנג אין דר'הויך, איז נאָר זײַן גיפט,
דעם איבעריקן איז באַשערט צו וואַלגערן אַף דר'ערד זיך.

ער וועט ניט אויפהייבן זיך העכער פונעם קיווער-גראָז,
וואָס אונטער דעם — די זיגן זײַנע מערן זיך און מערן ;
אַהין וועט ער מיט שווערד זיך קומען אויסקלינגען דעם ראָסט
און שפּײַזן אין דער פינצטער זיך אין איינעם מיט די ווערעם.

און אויסמעסטן מיט זיי זיך אין דער גרעב,
און אין דעם גראָד, און אין דעם גיר, און אין דעם עקל ;
אַלץ איינס — צי האָט ער דיר אַ לאַטע צוגעקלעפּט,
אַנשטאָט די שאַנד די אייגענע מיט איר פאַרדעקן.

Then wear it, homeless one, don't lose hold of your senses,
Why should you care—what's covering the taken and the naked?
Perhaps some day the two of you will have the chance
To draw swords against the Golem—as in a bull-fight.

27

Let it not weigh upon you—the yellow patch,
Nor be ashamed, my homeless one, of your tangled hair.
Walk straight, as did your grandfather and father,
To the roads of dawn someday you will be known.

Known also to the crossroads, my beloved,
In the place where once—head lifted high with pride—
Against the darkness there rose up Akiva
And his farthest descendants—tempered hard as steel.

The Golem follows you. It does not tally,
That age-old accounting of his apelike brain;
That you should have to pay him for the yellow patch, —
He thought about it for two thousand years.

For he'd sowed nothing else with his own hands,
He reaped and stored just the fruits of strangers' toil;
—Walk straight, my homeless one, like your grandfather and father,
The roads of dawn will ever know of you.

28

Will you not, someday, take flight again, my homeless one?
Is there a road that has not felt your pain and grief?
Brest-Litovsk was opened up like an ancient tome
And hordes come, laden with lament and sorrow.

On foot. Hunched over. With children in their arms.
The beards—lifted up, where else but to the stars.
The *goles*[9]—tied to their loins with knotted belts,[10]
And parchment brows are strained with speculation.

Their mouths warmed by the flickering lights of candles,
They seat themselves, as for *shive*,[11] on the ground;
The winds are howling: —Who'll have pity on them?
And sometimes a star comes running through, like a sword.

9. *goles*: Diaspora, or Dispersion.
10. Worn during prayer by religious Jews.
11. *shive*: In the week of mourning, Jews sit on low benches.

נו, טו זי אָן, מײַן הײמלאָזע, און זיך פון זין ניט ריר,
אַ דײַגע דיר — מיט וואָס ס'פּאַרדעקן זיך באַנומענע און הוילע?
ס'וועט עפּשער נאָך אַמאָל דיר אויסקומען מיט איר,
ווי אין אַן אָקסנשלאַכט — זיך פעכטן קעגן גוילעם.

.27

ניט שוווער זאָל זי דיר זײַן — די געלע לאַטע,
ניט שעם זיך, הײמלאָזע, מיט די צעלאָזטע האָר.
גײן גלײַך, ווי ס'איז געגאַן דײַן זיידע און דײַן טאַטע,
דערקאָנען וועלן דיך די וועגן פון קאַיאָר.

דערקאָנען וועלן דיך די קרײַצוועגן, מײַן ליבע,
וואָס איבער זיי — דעם קאָפּ פאַרהויבן שטאָלץ —
קעגן דער פינצטערניש געגאַנגען איז אַקיווע
און זײַנע ווײַטסטע אָפּשטאַמען — פאַרהאַרטעוועט, ווי שטאָל.

דער גוילעם גײט דיר נאָך. עס שטימט ניט אַקוראַט דאָ
דער אַלטער כעזשבן אין זײַן מאַלפּישן געהיר;
באַצאָלן נאָך עפּעס דו דאַרפסט אים פאַר דער געלער לאַטע, —
ער האָט דאָך צוויי יאָרטויזנט געקלערט אָף איר.

ער האָט מיט הענט מיט זײַנע עפּעס אַנדערש ניט געזייט דאָך,
ער האָט דאָך בלויז פון פרעמדע מי געשניטן און געשפּאָרט;
— גײ גלײַך, מײַן הײמלאָזע, ווי ס'איז געגאַן דײַן טאַטע און
דײַן זיידע,
דערקאָנען וועט אַ יעדער וועג דיך פון קאַיאָר.

.28

ווײסטו נאָך ווידער, ווען עס איז, מײַן הײמלאָזע, אַ פּלי טאָן?
איז נאָך פאַראַן אַ וועג, וואָס ווייסט ניט פון דײַן ווינט און ווײ?
געעפנט האָט זיך, ווי אַן אַלטער סייפער בריסק-דעליטע
און ס'קומען מענגעס אַנגעלאָדענע מיט טרויער און געוויין.

צופוס. געהויקערטע. מיט קינדער אָף די הענט.
די בערד — אינדר'הויך. די ריכטונג — לויט די שטערן.
דער גאָלעס — אײַנגעקנופּט מיט גאַרטלען צו די לענד,
אָף כקירע רײַסן זיך די פאַרמעטענע שטערנס.

באַ שטיקלעך צאַנקענדיקע ליכט די מײַלער זיך דערוואָרעמען
זיך אויסגעזעצט זיי האָבן, ווי צו שיווע אָף דער ערד;
און ווינטן וואָיען: — ווער וועט זיך אָף זיי דערבאַרעמען?
און אַלע ווײַל לויפט דורך אַ שטערן, ווי אַ שווערד.

From the river Bug—an insane blizzard rages,
With its whipping snow, it wipes out every footstep;
And from the twisted menorahs of the Bialystok synagogues,
They hung the *goles,* like some hanging fiddles.

29

A crumb of bread at alien thresholds—even a dry one—
How many times have you had to part at thresholds?
And now that you have come into my heart,—
I will not ask you—from where or where to . . .

You are dancing out the pain of generations,
And from your joints it's wildly striving to break free;
—Who could have guessed it's your desperate way of flight?
—And who could have known at the flayed Vistula?

The Jordan cut your feet, as if with glass
And Babylon's rivers overflowed with your tears,
And when they left you by the Rhine in flames
Did not the Kremlin's stars ascend for you?

Let now my heart be for you, like a nest in a tree,
While yet no axe has felled the tree to earth;
You must still dance out the shame-dance of Sodom,
My abandoned one, my sorrowing queen.

30

On every road where you were hunted, driven,
I gather what your quiet steps had sown;
And I will bind them into forlorn sheaves
So that I may hoist them on my back with joy:

This is what I possess from your two thousand years,
Only your blazing feet that, through pain and sorrow,
Like drumming drums will drum away,
And like the drums—they'll keep on drumming.[12]

I burrow beneath the ruined nests,
And I wake up your sorrow from its sleep;
And I will learn by heart the songs of birds
So I can sing you back to sleep on an unfamiliar road:

12. From a Yiddish folk song, called, "*Az der Rebe Elimelech . . .*" —When the rabbi becomes happy, he calls for his drummers, his fiddlers, etc.

פון בוג דעם טײַך — אַ זאַווערוכע בושעוועט אַ דולע,
פאַרווישט אַ יעדן טראָט דאָרט, שמײַסנדיק מיט שניי;
נאָר אַף געבויגענע מענוירעס פון די ביאַליסטאָקער שולן
דעם גאָלעס, גלײַך ווי פידלען אויפגעהאנגען האָבן זיי.

.29

אַ ברעקל ברויט באַ פרעמדע שוועלן — אַ פאַרדאַרטס. —
שוין וויפל מאָל האָסטו אַף שוועלן זיך געזעגנט?
אַצינדערט אָנגעקומען ביסטו אין מײַן הארץ, —
איך וועל — פונוואַנען און וווּהין — באַ דיר ניט פרעגן...

עס טאַנצט אַ דוירעסדיקע פײַן פון דיר אַרויס,
פון דײַנע אָנגלען רײַסט זי ווילד איצט אַף דער פרײַ זיך;

— ווער האָט באַשיידט, אַז ס'איז דײַן העפקערער וועג-אויס?
— ווער האָט געפּאַסקנט באַם געפּאַסעוועטן ווײַסל?

די פּיס געשניטן האָט דער יאַרדן דיר, ווי גלאָז
און באָוולס טײַכן זיך פאַרפלײַצט מיט דײַנע טרערן,
און ווען באַם ריין האָט מען מיט פײַער דיך געלאָזט
זײַנען ניט אויפגעגאַנגען דען פאַר דיר די קרעמלדיקע שטערן?

זאָל איצט מײַן הארץ דיר, ווי אַ נעסט זײַן אַף אַ בוים,
קאָלזמאַן די האַק האָט נאָך דעם בוים ניט אומגעוואַלגערט;
דו דאַרפסט נאָך אויסטאַנצן דעם בושע־טאַנץ פון סדוים,
מײַן העפקערע,מײַן טרויעריקע מאַלקע.

.30

אַף יעדן וועג, ווו מ'האָט געיאָגט דיך און געטריבן,
פון שטילע טריט דײַנע איך זאַמל דעם פאַרזיי;
איך וועל אין גאַרבן זיי צונויפבינדן אין טריבע
צום אָנטאָן פריילעך אַף די אַקסל וועל איך זיי:

— אָט דאָס פאַרמאָג איך פאַר יאָרטויזנטיקן דײַגען,
נאָר דײַנע בליצנדיקע פּיס אַף ווינד און ווײי
וועלן ווי פײַקלדיקע פײַקלעך זיך צעפײַקלען
און וועלן פײַקלדיקע — פײַקלען וועלן זיי.

אונטער די כאָרעוודיקע נעסטן זיך פאַרלייג איך,
דעם אײַנגעשלאָפענעם דעם ווײי דײַנעם איך וועק;
איך וועל זיך אויסלערנען די לידער פון די פייגל
און דיך פאַרוויגן אַף אַן אומבאַקאַנטן וועג:

Nothing else do I possess, my weary homeless one,
Only your hands, which are stifling such a scream;
They're fiddling away just like the fiddling fiddles,
And like the fiddles—they'll keep on fiddling.

31

Without a home, without a roof, without a road,
Without succor or consolation, without words, —
But the whole earth will be awakened by your feet,
And only your thirsts—unquenched and unextinguished.

A scarlet forest is lost upon your shoulders,
Like waves of fire in a blaze—they're stooped;
Over such a flame my mother blessed the candles,
While covering with her hands her tearful eyes.

So move lightly along the precipice's edge,
As winds lament you on their mournful flutes;
You must still dance out the age-old shame,
You must still dance out the age-old ancestral pain.

The day—quite shaken—like a sack carried on your body,
Above your head—the swastika is unfurled;
—There is no sword that was not sharpened on you,
—There is no sword that will not shatter on you.

32

Would then my heart, my solitary one, suffice
For weeping out the pain, for arguing out the complaint?
I heard how the river Bug was weeping over you,
When you were dancing for the ones who had tortured you.

—Something merry!—they gave an order to the wind,
Those evil ones, they drove your wander-feet into a frenzy;
The frost, it served them as an icy whip,
And how the snow was whirling in white madness.

From my eyes the procession will never fade,
Nor from the plucked out eyes with their frozen tears;
—Who saw how the night was bearing you to be devoured
In the glistening teeth of the unblushing stars?

כ׳פֿאַרמאָג מער גאָרנישט ניט, מײַן הײמלאָזע, מײַן מידע,
נאָר דײַנע הענט, וואָס האַלטן אײַן אַזאַ געשרײ
וועלן, ווי פֿידלדיקע פֿידלען זיך צעפֿידלען
און וועלן פֿידלדיקע — פֿידלען וועלן זײ.

.31

אָן אַ הײם און אָן אַ דאַך, און אָן אַ וועג,
אָן אָן אָנלען ,אָן אַ טרײַסט און אָן אַ לאַשן, -
נאָר גאָרע ערד ווערט פֿון די טריט דײַנע דערוועקט
און דײַנע דאָרשטן — ניט געשטילט און ניט געלאַשן.

אַ רויטער וואַלד אָף דײַנע אַקסלען זיך פֿאַרלירט,
ווי כוואַליעס פֿײַער אין אַ סרײפֿע — אויסגעבויגן;
אָף אַזאַ פֿײַער האָט געבענטשט מײַן מאַמע ליכט,
מיט פֿינגער צוגעדעקט די ווײנענדיקע אויגן.

איז טראָג זיך, טראָג איבער דעם אָפּגרונטיקן ראַנד,
ס׳באַקלאָגן ווײנטן דיך אָף טרױעריקע פֿלײַטן;
דו דאַרפֿסט נאָך אויסטאַנצן אַ דוירעסדיקן שאַנד,
דו דאַרפֿסט נאָך אויסטאַנצן אַ דוירעסדיקן ווײטיק.

ד׳ער טאָג — צעבויטעט — ווי אַ זאַק איז אָף דײַן לײַב,
איבער דײַן קאָפּ — די האָק און קרײַץ זײַנען צעפֿעכערט;
— ניטאָ די שווערד, וואָס האָט אָף דיר זיך ניט געשלײַפֿט,
— ניטאָ די שווערד, וואָס וועט אָף דיר זיך ניט צעברעכן.

.32

ווײט דען מײַן האַרץ מײַן אײנציקס זײַן געגנוג
אָף אויסווײנען דעם ווײ, אָף אויסטײַנען די טײַנע?
איך האָב געהערט, ווי ס׳האָט געווײנט אָף דיר דער בוג,
ווען האָסט געטאַנצט פֿאַר זײ, וואָס האָבן דיך געפֿײַניקט.

— אַ פֿרײלעכס! — האָבן זײ באַפֿוילן צו דעם ווינט,
און דײַנע וואַנדער-פֿיס געמאַרדעוועט זײ האָבן בײזע;
דער פֿראָסט האָט ווי אַ בײַטש זײ, ווי אַ פֿראַסטיקע געדינט
און ווי דאָס ווײַסע מעשוגאַס געוואָרפֿן האָט דער שנײ זיך.

פֿון מײַנע אויגן טרעט ניט אָפּ דער בלאָנדזשענדיקער צוג
און די אַרויסגעזעצטע אויגן מיט פֿאַרקילטע טרערן;
— ווער האָט געזען, ווי ס׳האָט די נאַכט געטראָגן דיך פֿאַרצוקט
אין בלײאַסקענדיקע צײַן פֿון אומפֿאַרשעמטע שטערן?

Would then my love repay you for your anguish?
And would my heart be able to sing out your woe?
Until heavens would spew flame and rocks upon them,
Until their cities would go dancing in a death-dance.

33

Lull him to sleep, the wanderer, with your dancing,
Lull him so quietly to sleep along the way;
You've already taken leave of all you had
And now you must bid farewell also to him.

Take your leave, while dancing—exactly so.
It does not matter, that your naked feet are twisting;
The leaves on the trees are ashamed of being green,
And the snow on the ground is choking on its whiteness.

Your fluttering footsteps I behold from afar
And each one makes itself a quiet space in my heart:
If you want to take along the wind—take it.
There's heart enough. There are enough spaces in it.

He does not fall asleep, the wanderer,
He weeps, as rain weeps in the middle of the night.
So let him weep. You've taken leave of all you had,
And now you must bid farewell also to him.

34

—Whom else would you want to take along with you?
—What else do you wish to bring into my heart?
Blossoms then the tree in spring from sun and dew,
As my own heart blossoms from thirsting and from yearning?

The sea had spread out far its shelf of blue,
Each little cloud the wind chased from the sky,
The stars, they burn so brightly in the night,
Would that I could conjure you, my beloved.

No roar do I hear out of the ocean's depths,
Without a sound the waves are racing towards the shore, —
They awaken me, they call to me, when a ship is passing by:
—Did I not have the urge to come out to the shore?

ווּעט דען מײַן ליבע דיר באַצאָלן פאַר דעם פּײַן?
און אויסזינגען דעם ווי ווּעט דען מײַן האַרץ אומשטאַנד זײַן?
ביז ס׳ווּעט מיט פלאַם און שטיין דער הימל זיי באַשפּײַען,
ביז אין אַ טויטן־טאַנץ וועלן זיך שטעט בײַ זיי צעטאַנצן.

.33

פאַרוויג אים, טאַנצנדיק, דעם נאַ־וועגנאַד,
פאַרשלעפּער שטיל אים אַף די וועגן;
מיט אַלץ געזעגנט האָסטו זיך, וואָס האָסט געהאַט
און איצט מיט אים אַליין זיך אויך געזעגן.

געזעגן, טאַנצנדיק זיך — אַקוראַט.
עס מאַכט ניט אויס, וואָס הויל די פּיס דײַנע זיך דרייען;
אַף ביימער גרין זײַן אַ ביזאַיען איז דעם בלאַט
און מיט דער ווײַסקייט וואַרגן זיך אַף דר׳ערד די שנייען.

צום פּאַך פון דײַנע טריט פון ווײַטנס איך פאַרנעם:
און יעדער גיט עפּעס אין האַרץ אַזאַ מין שטילן רוים מיר:
— אויב מיטנעמען דעם ווינט דיר ווילט זיך — נעם,
ס׳ווּעט קלעקן קלעקן האַרץ. פאַראַן גענוג זײַנען דאַרט רוימען.

ער שלאָפט ניט אײַן, דער נאַ־וועגנאַד,
ער וויינט, ווי ס׳וויינט אין מיטן נאַכט אַ רעגן.
איז זאָל ער וויינען. האָסט מיט אַלץ געזעגנט זיך, וואָס האָסט געהאַט
און איצט מיט אים אַליין זיך אויך געזעגן.

.34

— אַ ווּעמען נאָך וואָלסטו זיך מיטנעמען געוואָלט? — פאַרטרוי;
— וואָס וואָלסטו נאָך פאַרלאַנגט צו מיר אין האַרצן ברענגען?
בליט דען אַ בוים אין פרילינג פון דער זון און טוי,
ווי ס׳בליט מײַן האַרץ פון דאַרשטן און פון בענקען?

דער יאַם האָט אויסגעשפּרייט זײַן בלויע פּאַך,
אַ יעדער וואָלקנדל פון הימל האָט דער ווינט פאַרטריבן,
און שטערן ברענען אַזוי העל באַנאַכט,
זאָלסט זיך מיר קאָנען אויסדוכטן, מײַן ליבע.

ניט קיין געברום איך הער פון יאַמעדיקער טיף,
ניט מיט געדרויש צו ברעגן רײַסן זיך די כוואַליעס, —
זיי וועקן מיך, זיי רופן מיך, ווען ס׳גייט פאַרבײַ אַ שיף:
— צי כ׳וואָלט צום ברעג אַרויסגיין ניט געווען קיין באַלן?

—Of course. At once. Not an instant will I tarry.
No wind in the field can ever catch up with me;
Yet it seems that the ship is only passing by
And nothing more. It only touched the horizon . . .

35

The ship, it did not stop at the shore,
It seems to me, it was no ship at all;
It was only the road, so mournful and so dear, —
With all due respect, I would have made it even longer.

But perhaps instead I just might have imagined,
That a harbor had opened up amidst the stars;
I know, —not at the horizon, no, not there.
We need to come together, dearest one . . .

Such kind of feeling must the birds possess,
Who meet each other up in the sky so freely,
That if one of them were delayed along the way,
No way at all could they not find each other.

Yet to be parting is so very sad,
And such a gloom descends upon the borders;
It gives one to suck a taste of bitterness,
As when wings are spreading out before a flight . . .

36

Someone put out the light within the room,
So that I may see you better, my closest, my distant one . . .
But I don't begrudge myself a kind of sweetness in the pain, —
I shut fast my eyes—thirsty and purified.

I imagine that I'm climbing up a mountain,
Eyes—shut, so that I should not see the bottom.
—Is it not also worth my while to fall
From such a height, for you had soaked it in your honey?

Yet every step into the darkness does remind me
That we two are bound together—each to each;
The road is beckoning us, just like an outstretched hand, —
—How good it is, that no distance can separate us?

Yet never does the precipice release me,
Now is the peak itself bewitched. Doomed.
—For whom so mournfully do you let drop your head?
—For whom do you dance now, my golden one, my bride?

— אוואַדע. שוין. קיין רעגע כ'וועל ניט זאַמען.
קיין ווינט אין פעלד דעריאָגן ט'מיך ניט קאָנען;
נאָר ס'גייט די שיף ערגעץ אַדורך פאַרבײַ
און גאָרניט מער. דעם ראַנד פון הימל רירט זי אָן נאָר...

.35

ניט אָפּגעשטעלט האָט זיך די שיף באַם ברעג,
עס איז קיין שיף, מיר דוכט, אינגאַנצן ניט געווען גאָר;
עס איז נאָר טרויעריק און זיס געווען דער וועג, —
בעקאָוועד גאָדל וואָלט איך אים אַזוי פאַרלענגערט.

ס'וועט עפּשער אויסדוכטן מיר דאָך,
אַז אויפגעעפנט האָט צווישן די שטערן זיך אַ האָפן;
איך וויים, — ניט באַ דעם הימל־ראַנד, ניט דאָרט.
באַגעגענען זיך, ליבסטע, מיר באַדאַרפן...

ס'מוז אַ געפיל באַ פייגל זײַן אַזאַ,
ווען זיי באַגעגענען זיך אַף דער פרײַ דאָרט,
אַז ווי ס'זאָל יעדערער ניט זײַן אין וועג פאַרזאַמט,
וועלן שוין איינס דאָס אַנדערע אינערגעץ זיך ניט מײַדן...

דאָך זיך געזעגענען איז טרויעריק אַזוי,
מיט אַזאַ אומעט דעקן איבער זיך די ראַנד;
עס גיט מיט ביטערקייט דאָס זיך אַ פאַרזויג,
ווען פליגל צו דעם אָפּלי שפּרייטן זיך פאַנאַנדער...

.36

אין צימער אויסגעלאָשן עמעץ האָט די שײַן,
איך זאָל דיך בעסער זען, מײַן נאָענטע, מײַן ווײַטע...
נאָר איך פאַרגין זיך ניט אַזאַ מין זיסן פּײַן, —
פאַרריגל איך די אויגן — דאַרשטיק און געליטערט.

מיר דוכט זיך אויס, אַז אַף אַ בארג ערגעץ איך שטײַג.
די אויגן — צו. איך זאָל קיין אָפּגרונט ניט דערקאָנען.
— צי איז אַראָפּפאַלן דען אויכעט ניט קעדײַ
פאַר אַזאַ הייך, וואָס איז פאַרזויגן מיט דײַן האָניק?

נאָר יעדער טראָט אַדורך דער פינצטערניש דערמאָנט,
אַז צוגעבונדן — איינס צו איינס — מיר זײַנען ביידע;
עס ציט דער וועג זיך, ווי אַן אויסגעשטרעקטע האַנט, —
— ווי גוט עס איז, וואָס ס'קאָן קיין שטרעקע ניט צעשיידן?

עס לאָזט דער אָפּגרונט איצט אין ערגעץ מיך ניט אָפּ,
עס איז די הייך אַליין פאַרקישעפט איצט. פאַרפאַלן.
— פאַר וועמען פאַלט איצט אַזוי טרויעריק דײַן קאָפּ?
— פאַר וועמען טאַנצסטו איצט, מײַן גאָלדענע, די קאַלע?

37

Along the seashore magnolia has blossomed
And its juices are telling fortunes at every threshold;
I know not, who fettered tight my shoulders,
I know not who it was, who stopped up my very breath.

The borders call to me—rounded and rosy,
Each little breeze confides to me its secrets;
It seems to me, that I am circling around as in a siege,
And that each road returns me hurryingly home.

And at home, somebody piles on top of me,
He wakes me up and drives me from my bed;
Yet no one hears when the door is opened wide, —
And outside there's pitch darkness and it's raining . . .

Through the pouring rain I hear your voice, my homeless one,
Your quiet, stifled weeping, I hear, my love,
As I hear your aroma in the flowering magnolia,
As I hear your sad steps inside my heart . . .

38

You're far away, my homeless one, you're far away, my love, —
Are you putting on your wedding gown now for dancing?
Are you covering your moonlit body with it now,
Like a naked sword enclosed within its sheath?

The Kazbek shall rise today from earth's foundations,
Its silvery head will not be able to find out—
If a wayward wind had departed from it,
Or if at its foot the blue snow still is raging?

In your flight you will see neither it nor anyone,
When you will have been sucked dry of life by love;
But the world of ancient times will be revealed to you,
To those sealed-up eyes of yours, so full of grief.

And I will then be sitting by the seashore,
Tossing pebbles to drive away the sadness,
And waiting for a letter, that you should write me—don't delay,
Saying— "After the dance I did not come to you today" . . .

.37

ס'האָט דער מאַגנאַלי אַרום יאַם זיך שוין צעוואַקסן
און זײַנע זאַפּטן פאַרוואַראַזשען יעדער שוועל;
איך ווייס ניט, ווער עס האָט געפּענטעט מײַנע אַקסל,
איך ווייס ניט, ווער עס האָט דעם אָטעם מיר פאַרשטעלט.

די ראַנדן רופן מיך — פאַררויטלטע און רונדע,
ס'גיט יעדער ווינטל עפּעס איבער מיר געהיים;
ווי אין באַלאַגערונג איך גיי, דאַכט זיך, אַרום דאָ,
אַ יעדער וועג קערט אום מיך אײַליק צוריק אַהיים.

און אין דער היים וואַלגערט זיך אַן עמעץ אָף מיר,
ער וועקט מיך אויף און יאָגט אַראָפּ מיך פון געלעגער;
עס הערט ניט קיינער, ווי ס'צעעפנט זיך די טיר, —
און ס'איז אין דרויסן אַזאַ כווישעך און אַ רעגן...

איך הער, מיין הימלאַזע, אין רעגן־גאַס דײַן קאָל,
דײַן שטיל געוויין, דײַן אײַנגעהאַלטנס, כ'הער, מײַן ליבע,
ווי כ'הער דײַן רייעך אינעם בליִענדן מאַגנאָל
ווי כ'הער די טריט דײַנע אין הארץ מײַנעם, די טריבע...

.38

ביסט ווײַט, מײַן הימלאָזע, ביסט ווײַט, מײַן ליבע, —
צי טוסטו איצט ניט אָן צום טאַנצן דײַן קאָלע־קלייד?
צי דעקט דײַן מוילעד־לײַב מיט דעם אַצינד זיך איבער,
ווי ס'דעקט אַ הוילע שווערד זיך איבער מיט אַ שייד?

ס'וועט הײַנט זיך אויפהייבן פון גרונט־פעסט דער קאַזבעק,
זײַן קאָפּ זײַן זילבערנער ניט קאָנען וועט באַשיידן —
צי איז אַ ווינט אַ העפקערער פון אים אַוועק,
צי אין דער נידער בושעוועט זײַן בלויער שניי דאָרט?

וועסט אים ניט זען און קיינעם ניט אין דײַן געיעג,
ווען אויסגיין וועסט פון ליבע אויסגעזויגן;
נאָר ס'וועט די גאַנצע אורוועלט זײַן פאַר דיר אַנטפּלעקט,
פאַר די פאַרריגלטע, פאַר דײַנע טרויעריקע אויגן.

און איך וועל זיצן בײַ דעם ברעג פון יאַם,
מיט שטיינדלעך אָפּטרײַבן פון זיך דעם אומעט
און וואַרטן אָף אַ בריוו, דו זאָלסט מיר שרײַבן — ניט פאַרזאַמט,
אַז — „נאָך דעם טאַנץ בין איך צו דיר הײַנט ניט געקומען"...

39

Only you, my peahen, like the golden dawn,
After long waiting, I surely hope one day to see you;
The sun will rise then with the blazing of your hair,
And bearing pure saffron, the new day will leap forth.

For you I shall set out such beguiling spells,
Like food that is set out for birds in feeders;
They'll intoxicate you like a suckling babe,
And make you forget your far-flung trail of woe . . .

No gold have I to forge for you a shrine,
But from my heart I'll weave for you a nest of sounds;
In the flaming of your hair in the farthest places,
I'm imprisoned alone as in a golden cage.

It's dawn already. The birds are just waking up
With such a joyful twittering and bustling;
And I am setting out to meet you—up the mountain,
I'll patiently await you there, my golden one, my peahen.

40

The sea is quiet and fair are all the days,
I see you like a sailboat tossed upon the billows;
A kindly wind will bring you to the shore
And bid farewell to you at thresholds of pure gold.

The wind, it will be taking leave of you
And forever will conclude with *Shmuel-Alef.*[13]
—Stay . . . put forth roots . . . grow green anew,
And bid farewell forever to your sorrow.

Here the earth to each and every one is faithful,
Here even the driest roots shall bloom anew, —
Here the sapling tree will be a kinsman to you,
Here every grain of sand will be a mother to you . . .

The sea is quiet and mightier than wine,
I see you like a seagull soaring along the shore;
—My homeless one, my beloved, —come inside,
Here our childhood waits for us with raisins and almonds . . . [14]

(1940)

13. *Shmuel-Alef*: The Biblical Book of Samuel I.
14. The motif of "raisins and almonds" (*rozhinkes un mandlen*) is found in many Yiddish folk songs.

.39

נאָר דיך, מײַן פאַווע, ווי דעם גאָלדענעם קאַיאָר,
וועל איך געווים זיך, וואַרטנדיק דערוואַרטן;
די זון וועט אויפגיין מיטן פלאַם פון דײַנע האָר,
מיט פרישן זאַפרען וועט דער טאָג אַזאַ מין שפּאַר טאָן.

כ׳וועל פאַר דיר אויסלייגן פאַרשפּרעכונגען אַזוי,
ווי שפּײַז מע לייגט אַף ווענטקעס פאַר די פייגל;
ס׳זאָל מיט פאַרשיקערונג דיך געבן אַ פאַרזויג
און דיך פאַרגעסן מאַכן אין דײַן ווײַטן ווײ־גאַנג . . .

כ׳האָב ניט קיין גאָלד אַף אויסשמידן פאַר דיר אַ שטיין,
כ׳וועל פון מײַן האַרץ אַ נעסט נאָר אויסוועבן אין קלאַנגען;
אין פלאַם פון דײַנע האָר אַף גאָרע שטרעקעס ווײַט,
בין איך אַליין, ווי אין אַ שטײַג אַ גאָלדענער געפאַנגען.

ס׳איז שוין קאַיאָר. די פייגל הייבן זיך שוין אויף
מיט אַזאַ גליקלעך־צוויטשענדיקן האַווען;
איך לאָז אַנטקעגן דיר אַרויס זיך — באַרג אַרויף,
כ׳וועל דיך דערוואַרטן זיך, מײַן גאָלדענע, מײַן פאַווע.

.40

דער יאַם איז שטיל און העל זײַנען די טעג,
כ׳זע ווי אַ זעגל־שיף דיך בלאָנדזשען איבער וועלן;
עס וועט דיך צופירן דער גוטער ווינט צום ברעג
און זיך געזעגענען מיט דיר בײַ גינגאָלדענע שוועלן.

געזעגענען מיט דיר וועט זיך דער ווינט
און מיט שמועל־אַלעפן אַף שטענדיק זיך געשלאָסן.
— פאַרבלײַב . . . פאַרפלאַנץ זיך . . . ווער פונסנײַ באַגרינט.
געזעגן זיך אַף שטענדיק מיטן טרויער.

דאָ איז די ערד אַ יעדערן געטרײַ,
דאָ בליִען אויף די אויסגעדאַרטסטע שטאַמען, —
דאָ וועט דיר יעדער ביימל זײַן אַ פרײַנט,
דאָ וועט דיר יעדער זעמדל זײַן אַ מאַמע . . .

דער יאַם איז שטיל און קרעפטיקער פון ווײַן,
כ׳זע ווי אַ מעווע דיך אַרומשוועבן בײַ ראַנדן;
— מײַן היימלאָזע, מײַן ליבע, — קום אַרײַן,
די קינדהײַט וואַרט אונדז דאָ מיט ראָזשינקעס און מאַנדלען . . .

.1940

THE HOSPITABLE BIRD

I

It did not waken him, the noise
Of falling leaves at summer's end;
For he came out alone on foot
To welcome his own lonely sadness . . .

A sunflower—badly broken up;
A bee is circling round it, buzzing:
It flies—first one way, then—the other.
How does it look right here, the sadness?

Where it broke off the break was straight.
The autumn strew it everywhere;
And from the wind, a silent cry, —
And is that how it looks, the sadness?

The leaf-filled glade is in full glory,
The trees are flying, perhaps sadly.
He looks around to every side:
—Now, how does it look, the sadness?

Quickly he stepped forth from afar,
And suckling, fastened unto me:
—The sadness it surely looks like me,
My sad, my hospitable bird.

Through falling leaves—up to his chest,
As through summer's golden shavings, —
He walks around on foot alone,
Bringing greetings to his sadness . . .

2

Perhaps, like all—in time of withering,
When autumn first demands its due, —
Its nest, it too fell down in shambles,
And in it, he—just like a widow? . . .

דער גאָסטפּריַינטלעכער פויגל

.1

ניט אויפגעוועקט האָט אים דער רויש
פון בלעטער־פאַל באַם ראַנד פון זומער;
ער איז אַליין צופוס אַרויס
מעקאַבל פּאָנעם זײַן דעם אומעט...

אַ זונענרויז — פאַרבראָכן, שווער;
אַ בין אַרום איר עפּעס זשומעט:
אַ וועג — אַ היין, אַ וועג — אַהער,
ווי זעט ער אויס אָט דאָ, דער אומעט?

פון בראָכע ברעכט זיך אײַן דער פליין.
צעשטעקט דער האַרבסט זי אומעטום האָט;
און פונעם ווינט אַ שטיל געוויין, —
צי זעט ער אויס אַזוי, דער אומעט?

דער לאָן אין בלעטער, ווי אין רום,
די ביימער פליִען, דאַכט זיך, אומעט;
ער קוקט אין יעדער זײַט זיך אום:
— ווי זעט ער פּאָרט דאָ אויס, דער אומעט?

אַ גיי געטאָן ער האָט אַף גיך,
פון ווײַט — אין מיר זיך אײַנגעזויגן:
— עס זעט דער אומעט אויס, ווי איך,
מײַן גוטער, גאָסטפּרײַנטלעכער פויגל;

אין בלעטער־פאַל — ביז צו דער ברוסט,
יוי נ׳סטרוזשקעס גאָלדענע פון זומער, —
גייט ער אַליין אַרום צופוס
מעקאַבל פּאָנעם זײַן דעם אומעט...

.2

קאָן זײַן, ווי אַלץ — אין צײַט פון וועלק,
ווען ס׳האָט דער האַרבסט גענומען מאָנען, —
איז אויך זײַן נעסט געוואָרן — טעל
און ער אין איר — ווי אַן אַלמאָנע?...

Perhaps, beneath the gust of rain,
When all is driven to undress, —
He too in nakedness remained
With nothing left him to show off . . .

Perhaps, as from the knife's sharp touch,
He could not save himself in autumn;
Possibly—he changed his color,
Possibly—his feathers changed . . .

Only his voice remained, and glance,
And pride of head, that keeps on swaying
In its scarlet downy hood
Over both his hovering wings.

Neither did he shed his tail,
Which, like a slick, adds sheen in summer.—
Thus he set out upon his way,
Bringing welcome to the sadness . . .

3

He scrutinizes every bush,
Where groaning twigs are bending over:
—And you shall also welcome me,
My hospitable, kindly bird:

For no sadness has the autumn,
Sweet weariness is on the roads;
I am he, whom you need so,
And you have rightly greeted me:

For there is no pain in withering,
Only a promise of rebirth;
O, not alone to you I come, —
I come with mountains, —with my kin:

The way to you is like a harp,
Laden with a thousand tones.
You're the one I also need,
As a seed has need of soil.

קאָן זײַן — אונטער דעם רעגן־קנויל,
ווען אַלץ געצוווּנגען איז זיך אויסטאָן, —
איז ער דאָן אויך געבליבן הויל
און האָט זיך ניט מיט וואָס אַ גרויס טאָן...

קאָן זײַן, אַז פון דעם מעסערם ריר
האָט זיך אין הארבסט ניט אויסגעהיט ער.
מעגלעך — געענדערט דעם קאָליר,
מעגלעך — די פעדערן געביטן...

נאָר ס׳קאָל ז׳געבליבן און דער בליק,
דער שטאָלץ פון קאָפּ, וואָס טוט זיך וויגן
אין רויטן פוכענעם באַשליק
איבער די שוועבנדיקע פליגל...

און ניט פאַרקירצט האָט ער דעם עק,
וואָס ווי אַ שליים באַשײַנט אים זומער. —
אַזוי איז ער אַרויס אין וועג
מעקאַבל פּאָנעם זײַן דעם אומעט...

3.

ער קוקט אין יעדן קוסט זיך אײַן,
ווו צווײַגן קרעכצנדע זיך בויגן:
— ווּעסט מ י ך מעקאַבל פּאָנעם זײַן,
מײַן גאַסטפרײַנטלעכער, גוטער פויגל:

ניטאָ קיין אומעט אין דעם הארבסט,
ס׳איז זיסע מידקייט אַף די וועגן;
און איך בין דער, ווּעמען דו דאַרפסט,
און ריכטיק האָסטו מיך באַגעגנט.

ניטאָ אין וועלקונג איז קיין ווײ,
פאַר ווידערוווּקס זי איז פאַרשפּראָכן;
אַ, ניט אַליין צו דיר איך גיי, —
איך גיי מיט בערג, — מיט מײַן מישפּאָכע:

דער וועג צו דיר איז, ווי אַ הארף,
מיט קלאַנגען טויזנטער געלאָדן.
און דו ביסט דער, ווּעמען איך דאַרף,
פּונקט ווי דער זאָמען דאַרף דעם באָדן.

Your welcome spreads over the earth,
—I'll be an echo to your song,
Though I don't wish to be your sadness.

(1947)

דײַן גאַסטפרײַנטשאַפט אַף ערד צעבליט,
— כ'וועל זײַן אַן אָפקלאַנג פון דײַן ליד,
נאָר איך פאַרלאַנג ניט זײַן דײַן אומעט.

.1947

AT DAYBREAK

Solemn like the dawn and weary—
A choppy sea itself caresses,
Listening to the smithy's clang
Through the bellows of green leaves.

It asks through little winds a question
With its tapestries of silver:
—Are there some bells along the road?
—A mountain spring is flowing by.

Overcome by its own clamor,
It listens in with silent wonder,
To the cricket's magic murmur,
To the cicada's frail stitching,

It spreads its plain before the stillness
At the last flicker of the green stars;
It hears, perhaps, that I'm awake,
That I go, a captive of the dawn . . .

(1948)

פאַרטאָג

פאַרטאָגיק-פֿייַערלעך און מיד —
צערטלט דער יאַם זיך, אַ געפּלעטער,
און הערט זיך אײַן, ווי ס׳קלינגט דער שמיד
באַם גרינעם בלאָז־זאַק פֿון די בלעטער.

ער גיט דורך ווינטעלעך אַ פֿרעג
מיט זײַנע זילבערנע געוועבן:
— ס׳איז ניט קיין גלעקלעך אויפֿן וועג?
— אַ באַרגנקוואַל פּליסט דורך דערנעבן.

פֿון רויש פֿון אייגענעם פֿאַרטשאַדעט,
הערט ער זיך אײַן פֿאַרוווּנדערט־שטיל
אין צויבער־מורמל פֿון דער גריל,
אין דינעם שטעפּ פֿון דער ציקאַדע.

פֿאַר שטילקייט איז געגרייט זײַן פֿלאַך,
פֿאַר לעצטן צאַנק פֿון שטערן גרינע;
ער הערט, עפּשער, ווי איך בין וואַך,
ווי כ׳גיי געפֿאַנגען אין באַגינען?...

.1948

THE SEA AT DAWN

The sea calls forth the calm of mountains
For its little nap at daybreak;
At its head—the flame of dawn;
At its feet—the twilight's mantle.

Waking with a start and groaning,
As if from dreaming, all atremble, —
Roused from sleep, it touches shore,
Tiny pebbles disarranging.

Trying then to grasp the shore,
It's caught in pebbles, as in a vise, —
There in the early morning's air,
There in the doze of early dawn.

Yet only the echo answers it
Of its own groaning—spreading out,
And on its moonlit lap descends
A trembling shadow from the shore.

(1948)

דער יאַם פאַרטאָג

די רו פון בערג פאַרופט דער יאַם
פאַר זײַן פאַרטאָגעדיקן דרעמל ;
צוקאָפּנס — פון באַגין דער פלאַם,
צופוסנס — אַ געהיל פון דעמער.

און מיט אַ קרעכצנדיקן וועק,
ווי דורך אַ כאָלעם אויפגעפלאַטערט, —
גיט ער פון שלאָף אַ טאַפּ דעם ברעג
און זײַנע שטיינדלעך אַ צעפּאַטל.

זיך אָנכאַפּן באַם ברעג ער פרוווט
און אין די שטיינדלעך זיך פאַרקלעמען
אין דער פרימאָרגעדיקער לופט,
אין דעם באַגינענדיקן דרעמל.

נאָר ס'ענטפערט אים מיט אָפּהילך בלויז
זײַן קרעכץ זײַן אייגענער — צעשאָטן
און ס'פאַלט אַף זײַן לעוואָנע־שויס
פון ברעג אַ ציטערדיקער שאָטן.

.1948

LENIN'S BAS-RELIEF

For this a sturdy brace of green
The stubborn mountain fir tree needs
To spread its branches for the bas-relief,
As does an eagle spread its wings.

For this the granite needs a hardness,
So the branches may be firmly rooted,
So time should not erase the figure
Carved with chisel and with hammer.

For this the mountains' height is needed,
For this, in beauty nature clothes itself,
To provide a worthy frame for him
Who is the reason for our being.

לענינס באַרעליעף

אַף דעם באַדאַרפט האָט גרינע העפט
די באַרגיקע, די אײַנגעשפּאַרטע יאָדלע.
זי זאָל די צווײַגן אויסשפּרייטן באַם באַרעליעף,
ווי ס׳שפּרייט די פליגל אויס אַן אָדלער.

אַף דעם באַדאַרפט האָט האַרטקייט דער גראַניט
און זײַן געוואָרצלט טיף מיט שטאַמען.
אַז ס׳זאָל די צײַט ניט אָפּווישן דעם שניט
וואָס איז פאַרקריצט פון דאָלעטע און האַמער.

אַף דעם באַדאַרפט די הויכקייט האָבן בערג
אַף דעם האָט אָנגעטאָן אין שיינקייט די נאַטור זיך.
אַז זײַן אַ ראַם זיי זאָלן זײַן די ווערט
פאַר דעם וואָס איז פון ז ײַ ן   די אורזאַך.

THE MOUNTAINS AT TWILIGHT

1

Their commanding shadows move the distance forward.
With heads—tossed back, like those of driven camels:
Only their wrinkled double chins are seen, —
They are dozing . . .

Perhaps of old, men bowed to them, as to some idols,
Laid sacrifices at their feet—young lambs;
But countless little paths cleverly smashed through them.
On golden hoops they stitched right through them . . .

A star falls down on them, but without a bit of light,
No thunder wakens them. No break can cause them pain:
And man alone is drawn to them—beguiled.
In them he sees—the chimera that is Genesis . . .

2

A rainbow is lacking in that frigid space,
To remind us solemnly about the Flood:
Let a mountain hitch onto it, as in a bridle,
Let another wrap it around, like a kerchief.

A flock of them descends, like a darkening cloud,
It drives the wind, while a swaying fir looks on;
The clouds are riding astride them, like white cowls,
And pass right through their heads, like whirling snow.

They embrace the horizon. And to the heavens—reach,
And send out their breezes to scout out each trail;
It seems: —that all at once they threw themselves up high;
As if they had to leap across the abyss . . .

3

In a golden hide—arrayed—
The mountains display themselves before the sunset,
As if they were preparing for a guest
From there, where stars are glowing.

די בערג פֿאַרנאַכט

.1

מיט שאָטנס שאָפֿן זיי די ווײַט פֿאַ ווים.
די קעפּ — פֿאַרדרייט, ווי בײַ פֿאַריאָגטע קעמלען:
מע זעט בײַ זיי די אויסגעקנייטשטע גיידערס בלויז, —
זיי דרעמלען...

כ׳האָט עפּשער, ווי צו געטער זיך צו זיי, געבוקט אַמאָל,
קאָרבאָנעס זיי געבראַכט צופֿוסנס — יונגע שעפּסן;
נאָר ס׳האָבן קלוגע סטעזשקעלעך געפּלעפֿט זיי אָן אַ צאָל.
מיט רייפֿן גאָלדענע אַדורכגעשטעפּט זיי...

אַ שטערן פֿאַלט אױף זיי, נאָר אָן אַ טראָפּן ליכט,
דער דונער וועקט זיי ניט. דער בראָך טוט זיי ניט ווײ שווין:
און נאָר דער מענטש זיך ציט צו זיי — פֿאַרפּירט.
ער זעט אין זיי — כימערן פֿון בערייִשים...

.2

אַ רעגנבויגן פֿעלט אין קאַלטן רוים,
ער זאָל דאָ פֿײַערלעך אין מאַבל אַ דערמאָן טאָן:
זיך אײַנשפּאַנען אין אים אַ באַרג זאָל ווי נ׳אַ צוים
און ווי אַ שטערנבאַנד — זאָל אים אַ צווייטער אָנטאָן.

נאָר ווי אַ כמאַרע נידערט שטיל אַ טשערעדע פֿון זיי,
זי טרײַבט דעם ווינט. ס׳קוקט אַ צעוויגטע יאָדלע אָן עם;

אַף זיך די וואָלקנס רײַטן זיי, ווי ווײַטע קאַפּושאָנעס
און שפּאַרן דורך די קעפּ, ווי פֿון אַ ווירבלדיקן שניי.

צום ראַנד זיי טוליען זיך. דעם הימל — אַ דערגרייך,
און ווינטלעך־אויסשפּירער אַף יעדן שטעג זיי וואַרפֿן;
עס דוכט: — זיי האָבן זיך אַ הייב געטאָן אינדר׳הייך,
פּונקט ווי דעם אָפּגרונט איבערשפּרינגען זיי באַדאַרפֿן...

.3

אין פֿעל אין גאָלדענע — באַצירט —
שטעלן די בערג זיך אויס צו שקיִע.
פּונקט ווי אַף געסט מ׳וואָלט זיך געריכט
פֿון דאָרט, ווו שטערן זיך צעגליִען.

Just then a mournful cow comes into view,
And lowers its horns down to the grass.
—A youthful shepherd—from out of nowhere—
And a stillness so divine—then later . . .

They are drawing shadows closer—
A whip. A little sack—nearby . . .
And the mountains bleakly gaze at them,
Right through the dark-red mist . . .

נאָר ס׳קומט אַן אומעטיקע קו
און לאָזט צום גראָז אַראָפּ די הערנער.
— אַ פּאַסטעכל — פון ערגעץ־וווּ
און שטילקייט געטלעכע — נאָכהער נאָך...

זיי שלעפּן שאָטנס נאָך אַהער
אַ בײַטש. אַ טאָרבעלע — דערנעבן...
און ס׳קוקן טריב אַף זיי די בערג,
אַדורך דעם טונקל־רויטן נעפל...

RED ROCKS

Because of them, also the nearby fir tree
Wins fame. As if she herself were red—in her own right.
And they? Just so: moss overgrown and swollen
Like giant mushrooms, —those rocks of red.

Out of the mist the rocks fling up their heads:
Is someone looking for them—in passing by?
—Here they come, the passers-by, so firm of step—
The fir tree points the way with beckoning branches.

It has shaken off the mist from its own green self,
As a horse shakes water droplets from its mane;
And waits—should someone pause beside the rocks
And want to immortalize himself by carving his name on it . . .

(Kislovodsk, 1947)

רויטע שטיינער

אין זייער זכות, איז אויך די יאָדלע, וואָס דערביַי
שוין אויך באַרימט. ווי רויט געווען וואָלט זי. — אַליין נאָר.
און זיי? אַזוי: מיט מאָך באַוואָקסן און צעביַילט,
ווי שוואָמען ריזיקע, — די רויטע שטיינער.

פון אונטער נעבל וואַרפן זיי אַרויס די קעפּ:
צי זוכט מען זיי ניט — אין פאַרביַיגיין?
— אָט זיַינען זיי. פאַרביַיגייער, געפּאַסט אין טרעפּ, —
וויַיזט אָן די יאָדלע מיט פּאַרופּנדיקע צוויַיגן.

זי האָט דעם נעבל אָפּגעטרייסלט פון איר גרינס אַליין,
ווי ס׳טרייסלט אָפּ אַ פערד די גריווע אונטער וואַסער־שטראָמען;
און וואַרט — ס׳זאָל עמעץ באַ די שטיינער בליַיבן שטיין
און זיך פאַרייביקן אַף איר מיט אויסקריצן דעם נאָמען...

קיסלאָוואָדסק, 1947.

(UNTITLED)

Crunching the grass that was wilted, the cow
Brought up again the cud she was chewing;
Her eyes—without budging, staring off in the distance, —
The green of the tree fanned her face of a sudden.

Little she knew that a tree may be prickly,
Little she noticed the needles for leaves;
Its leaves barely stirred by the dawn's little breezes, —
Half-dipped in gilt, a fir tree was standing.

The cow, coming near, took one sniff of the fir, —
It smells the green thing: what is not, what is there . . .
At once lifting her tail at the feeling of pain,
She started to pick up the fir with her horns.

A shove to the tree, with delight at the taste,
Dumbly she strains for a while both her ears;
Then afterward—baffled—on the trunk of the tree
Begins scratching her head right between its two horns.

As someone might say: —So it happened. So what?
It's only a scratch, but the expenses mount up . . .
And the young little shepherd kneaded his sack, —
Tapped it to see if he had enough bread.

(1947)

* * *

ס׳פֿאַרוויאַנעטע גראָז האָט געקײַעט די קו
צוריק דאָס צעקײַעטע גראָז איז געקראָכן;
די אויגן — קיין ריר, אינדערווײַטן זי קוקט, —
און גרינס פֿון אַ בוים האָט געטאָן איר אַ פּאַכע.

זי האָט ניט פֿאַרשטאַנען, ווי ס׳שטעכט זיך אַ בוים,
זי האָט ניט געזען אָנשטאָט בלעטער די נאָדלען;
באַוועגט פֿון פֿרימאָרגיקן ווינטעלע קוים, —
אױף העלפֿט איז באַגילדעט געשטאַנען אַ יאָדלע.

איז צוגאַן די קו. פֿון דער יאָדלע אַ שמעק
ס׳איז גרין און סע שמעקט, וואָס איז ניט, וואָס איז יאָ דאָ...
אַ הייב געטאָן טייקעף פֿון ווייטאָק דעם עק
געלאָזט אױף די הערנער זיך נעמען די יאָדלע.

אַ שטויס אין דעם בוים, זיך געקוויקט מיט דעם טאָם
און אָנגעשטרענגט שטיל אױף אַ ווײַל דאָס געהער נאָך;
דערנאָך — אַ געפּלעפּטע — גענומען אין שטאָם
זיך קראַצן דעם שטערן צווישן די הערנער.

ווי איינער רעדט: — מיילע. סע טרעפֿט זיך, איז ניט:
איז כאַטש מיט אַ קראַץ די הויצאָעס זיך דעקן...
און ס׳פּאַסטעכל האָט פֿאַר דער טאַרבע געקניט, —
ער האָט עס געטאַפּט, צי דאָס ברויט וועט אים קלעקן.

.1947

THE OLD RACING-MACHINE

Beneath the decay and grime still shone the blue
Of her gaudy youth, that betrothed her to the road,
Though shreds like tassels are hanging from her body,
As from an old threadbare and faded garment.

No longer does one wash from her the dirt,
Only the road itself is wrapped around her wheels;
And her withered skin is peeling off in places
While elsewhere on her leather patches whisper to each other.

But if folks were to mount her raucously, pell mell,
With her diverting sun-faded patches,
The tassels, like a horse's mane, will start to wave,
And like the legs of thoroughbreds, the wheels will start to quiver.

And she will crow, like someone being strangled,
As from inside her, the dust, like wings, fans out;
For somewhere sharpening roads are waiting in the mountains,
And hidden chasms somewhere have been unsealed.

And then—someone would likely want to outrun her,
If only a pair of oxen—hitched to a makeshift cart.
Alight is then her joy when, wildly swinging,
Her body—filled with wind, each time blares out a honk.

And filled with fright, the oxen jump aside
And cursing, the driver looks from under his straw hat;
A cloud of dust he sees, floating in the distance,
An old jalopy careening past with its golden-reeling bodies, —

She creaks, she groans, she's jumping out of her skin,
Dancing her jig in and out of perilous passes;
The tassels fly from her body into the air,
And through the traffic she whirls, as in a mazurka.

More in the air than on the ground,
More in bounding leaps than on the looping roads;
Dancing an ecstatic dance upon the mountains,
Very like an ancient mountain-dwelling witch.

די אַלטע רעיס־מאַשין

פון אונטער דער פאַרדאַרטער בלאָטע אַלץ נאָך בלויט
איר בונטע יוגנט, וואָס פאַרקנאַסט זי מיטן וועג האָט,
כאָטש ס'הענגען שוין אַריבער טראַלדן פון איר בויד,
ווי פון אַן אַלטן אָפּגעבליאַקעוועטן בעגעד.

מע וואָשט שוין מער ניט אָפּ פון איר דעם קויט,
אַרומגעוויקלט ליגט אַליין דער וועג אױף אירע רעדער;
עס שיילט זיך, ערטערוויַיז, איר דאַרע הויט
און ערגעץ שושקען זיך אויף איר די לאַטקעלעך פון לעדער.

נאָר אַז מע כאַפּט זיך אויף איר, טומלדיק, אַרויף
און מיט פאַרברוין פון זון די לאַטעס אַ פאַרעד איר,
גיבן די טראַלדן ווי אַ גריוווע זיך אַ פאַטער אויף,
ווי באַ אַ גוטן פערד די פים גיבן אַ ציטערל די רעדער.

און זי דערלאַנגט אַ קריי, ווי עמעצער וואָלט זי געוועַרגט,
אַ שטויב גיט אַ צעפּאַכע זיך פון איר, ווי פליגל;
עס וואַרטן ערגעץ שלייפנדיקע וועגן אין די בערג,
פאַרטיַיעט גיבן אָפּגרונטן זיך ערגעץ אַ צעזיגל —

און דאַן — אויך איר אַריבעריאָגן עמעצן זיך ווילט,
כאָטש אַ פאַר אָקסן — איַינגעשפאַנט אין אַ געביַי פון לאַזע;
די פרייד איז זוניק, אויפגעוויגט און ווילד,
די בויד — פאַרפולט מיט ווינט, גיט יעדער וויַיל אַ בלאָז זיך.

און אָקסן שפּרינגען אָפּ, דערשראָקן אין אַ זיַיט
און מיט אַ זידל קוקט פון אונטער שטרויען־הוט דער טריַיבער;
ער זעט אַ זיַיל פון שטויב, פאַרטראָגן אין דער וויַיט,
די דורכגעפלויגענע מאַשין מיט גאָלדיק־שווינדלדיקע ליַיבער, —

זי סקריפּעט און זי קרעכצט, און קריכט שוין פון דער הויט,
און טענצלט אונטער באַ געפערלעכע אַדורכגענג, —
עס פליִען אין דער לופט די טראַלדן פון איר בויד
און אַ פאַרקער זי וויכערט דורך, ווי אַ מאַזורקע —

מער אין דער לופט, ווי אויף דער ערד,
מער אין געשפּרונג, ווי אין די וועגעדיקע שלייפן;
זי טאַנצט, די בויד, אַריקעד אין די בערג,
גליַיך ווי אַ באַרגיקע אַן אַלטע מעכאַשייפע —

And above her boulders start to shake like drunkards,
And streaming rivers yield the way to her;
And whenever the precipices touch her,
Each time they give her a tickle with their rims.

She slows down then for doing further battle,
And perhaps again she'll scare a pair of oxen;
But from the other side—a second car is heard approaching,
It caroms past, blowing loudly like a *shofar*.[15]

A noise steals out from deep within the mountains,
A kind of driven weeping and a wail:
—Was this the darkness keening its lament,
Or did the mountains weep in their own darkness?

—Why do the mountains cry? Is it strange also to them,
The stillness of the skies? The cold of what is past?
The wind is surely fighting with the trees,
That somehow got stranded on that forsaken course . . .

Perhaps some forlorn person roams there too.
And night is falling, and the wind is unrelenting . . .
A low lament comes stealing in from the mountains
And while it's wailing, the lament vanishes too . . .

(1947)

15. A ram's horn, blown on some holidays in the synagogue.

און ס׳שאָקלען זיך, ווי שיקערע, די פעלדזן איבער איר,
און טײַכן שטראָמענדיקע טרעטן איר דעם וועג אָפּ;
ס׳גיט יעדער ווײַל דער אָפּגרונט זי אַ ריר,
אַ קיצל מיטן ראַנד ער גיט זי יעדער רעגע.

און לאָזט זי אָפּ פּאָר ווײַטערדיק געפּעכט,
און לאָזט זי נאָך אַמאָל דערשרעקן אַ פּאָר אָקסן;
נאָר פון אַנטקעגן — אַ מאַשין אַ צווייטע זיך דערהערט,
זי גיט מיט שויפעדיקן הילך אַ מעלדע און אַ טראָג זיך.

פאַרגאַנוועט פון אונטער די בערג אַ געריש זיך.
אַזאַ מין פאַריאָגטער געוואָי און געוויין:
— צי האָט זיך אַליין דאָרט צעיאָמערט דער כוישעך,
צי וויינען די בערג אין דער פינצטער אַליין?

— וואָס וויינען די בערג? איז זיי אויך דען אומהיימלעך
די שטילקייט פון הימל, די קעלט פון פאַרגאַנג?
עס שלאָגט פאַר געוויים זיך דער ווינט מיט די ביימלעך,
וואָס האָבן פאַרבלאָנדזשעט אין איינזאַמען גאַנג...

און עפּשער אַ מענטש דאָרטן בלאָנדזשעט פאַראיינזאַמט.
און ס׳פאַלט דאָרט די נאַכט, און ס׳פאַרפאַלגט דאָרט דער ווינט...
עס גאַנוועט אַרײַן פון די בערג דאָס געוויין זיך
און, וואָיענדיק, ערגעץ אַזוי סע פאַרשווינדט...

.1947

STAY, WIND, NEAR ME

Just seven years ago he reached his limit,
With restlessness and thirst he was fortified;
—Oh, wind, did you not see him? Nor any sign of him?
Yet even here the autumn was more than I could bear.

The pebbles on the beach. The mountains in their place.
The palm trees were the same, as always, as forever.
Yet only I have been gone for seven years
From back then, when I was here.

—Oh, wind, have you not seen them? —stay, wind, near me.
Time invades. How easily it does so.
Myself I surrender to it, bring it my heart, my striving,
Like bees, that bring their honey to the hive with love.

The work I spare her of weaving her own web,
Myself I surrender, running, into her arms, —
I hear the ringing echo, —not yet muted,
It rolls along the vanishing span of years.

Yes, it is I—in my continued vanishing;
Yes, it is I—a guest, I'm only passing through here;
I've reached my limit now. You see it, wind?
From it, I too shall inevitably depart.

(1948)

זײַ, װײנט, לעם מיר

דאָ איז מיט זיבן יאָר צוריק געװוען זײַן ראַנד,
מיט אומרו און מיט דאָרשט געפּעסטיקט ער געװוען איז;
— האָסט װײנט, אים ניט געזען? קײן סימען ניט פֿאַראַן?
דער האַרבסט אױך דאָ געבראָכן האָט מײַן גרענעץ.

די שטײנדלעך באַ דעם ברעג. די בערג אַף זײער אָרט.
די פּאַלמען פּונקט אַזױ, װי אַלעמאָל, װי שטענדיק,
נאָר איך בין אָפּגעטראָטן נאָך אַף זיבן יאָר
פֿון דאַן, װען כ'בין געװוען דאָ...

— האָסט, װײנט, זײ ניט געזען? — זײַ, װײנט, לעם מיר.
די צײַט באַפּאַלט. װי לײַכט ס'קומט אָן איר.
כ'גיב איר אַלײן זיך אױס. כ'טראָג איר מײַן האַרץ, מײַן מי,
װי נ'בינשטאָק טראָגט פֿאַרליבט די בין איר האָניק.

כ'פֿאַרשפּאַר אַלײן איר, װעבנדיק די נעץ,
אַלײן כ'גיב, לױפֿנדיק, זיך אַפּ אין אירע אָרעם, —
איך הער דעם גלאָקעדיקן הילך, — נאָך ניט געזעצט
ער קײַקלט זיך אַפּן פֿאַרשװינדנדיקן גאַנג פֿון יאָרן.

יאָ, דאָס בין איך — אין מײַן באַשטענדיקן פֿאַרשװינד,
יאָ, דאָס בין איך — אַ גאַסט איך גײ פֿאַרבײַ דאָ;
איצט איז אָט דאָ מײַן ראַנד. דו זעסט אים, װײנט?
אױך אָפּטרעטן פֿון אים כ'װעל אומפֿאַרמײַדלעך.

.1948

THE WINTER COMES

The winter did a message bring,
It whipped the fir trees, still so green
And rapidly, it shook their heads:
—The winter comes. It comes, the winter.

Perhaps someone did not quite complete his journey.
Will he after all succeed in reaching home?
Like bears, the mountains suck on their own paws
And trees are quivering as from a fever.

With a hullabaloo the message tears away
Fir tree after fir tree from the wind's mouth;
As if it were a calamity, the trees roil up
And with their needles raise a clatter.

The withered grass wakes up from sleep,
And withered leaves begin to thrash about
And everywhere are moans, and everything's in flux,
While the wind tries to scale the glossy walls.

It also summons to a dueling bout,
The barren trees, that all their leaves had shed:
But they are mute, they only shake their heads,
They only clap with their branches, as with bones.

(1948)

דער ווינטער גייט

גערבראַכט אַ בסורע האָט דער ווינט,
אַ שמייַעס געטאָן די יאָדלעס די צעגרינטע.
די קעפּ צעטרייסלט זיי געשווינט:
— דער ווינטער גייט. עס גייט דער ווינטער;

ס'האָט עפּשער נאָך זייַן וועג דאָרט ניט פאַרענדיקט ווער.
ווער נאָך באַווייַזן אָנקומען אַהיים ער?
ווי בערן זויגן לאַפּעס אייגענע די בערג
און ווי אין פיבער וואַרפן זיך דיביימער.

מיט אַ בעהאָלע רייַסט די בסורע אויס
באַם ווינט פון מויל אַ יאָדלע נאָך אַ יאָדלע:
זי גיבן זיך, ווי אַף אַן אומגליק אַ צעברויז
און אַ צעפּליעסקע מיט די נאָדלען.

עס כאַפּט זיך אויף דאָס טויטע גראָז,
אַ ריגעווע זיך געבן טויטע בלעטער
און אַלץ איז אַ געזוויין, און אַלץ איז אַ צעגאָס,
דער ווינט אַף ווענט אַף גלייַכע קלעטערט.

אַף אַ געפּעכט ער רופט דאָרט אויך אַרויס
די אָפּגעטרייסלטע, די הוילע ביימער:
זיי זייַנען שטום, מיט קעפּ זיי שאָקלען בלויז,
זיי קלאַפּן צו נאָר מיט די צווייַגן, ווי מיט ביינער.

1948.

THE ROSE

Fainted lay the rose upon the table,
Torn off just now from its thorny tangle:
—The first time in her life this had befallen her,
To sleep lying down. —What else could she do?

An early dew was still dripping from her.
And from her tiny narrow stem was hanging down
A little strip of green and peeling skin.
As if a garter went undone all of a sudden.

Two or three leaves—stretched out palms up—
Were lying around, like cast off clothes:
She sought them in her dream, this chopped-off rose.
And with her narrowed lips she breathed and stammered:

—Would she no longer open up at night?
—Would she no longer shut herself at dawn?
In her pink underwear she waited shivering
For her green foliage to cover her up.

But bent over now her little head is hanging.
As when in magic night, the nightingale serenades her.
And perched upon her slender stem she's looking down
Beneath the cloudy gusts of moonlit wind.

I am no nightingale: But I can give you back the dew.
I'll press you to my mouth. Perhaps again you'll blossom?
Till it hurts I'll give to you my breath—just so . . .
And . . . then blood suddenly spurted from my lips . . .

די רויז

פאַרכאַלעשט אַפן טיש געלעגן איז די רויז
אַ נאַר־וואָס אָפּגעריסענע פון דערנערדיקן פלאָנטער:
— דאָס ערשטע מאָל אין לעבן קומט איר אויס
צו שלאָפן ליגנדיק. — וואָס קאָן זי טאָן דען?

געטריפט האָט נאָך פון איר אַ פרישער טוי.
אַראָפּגעהאַנגען האָט פון שטענגעלע פון דינעם
אַ פּאַסיקל זיך שיילנדיקע גרינע הויט.
ווי ס׳וואָלט אַ זאָקנבענדל אָפּגעשפּיליעט זיך אינמיטן דרינען.

די צוויי־דריַי בלעטלעך — דלאָניעדיק געשטרעקט פאָרויס —
געוואַלגערט האָבן זיך, ווי איר צעוואָרפן אָנטאָן:
אין כאָלעם האָט זי זיי געזוכט, די אָפּגעהאַקטע רויז.
און מיט די דינע לעפעלך געאָטעמט און געפּלאָנטערט:

— וועט זי שוין מער ניט עפענען זיך אַף באַנאַכט?
— וועט זי שוין מער זיך ניט פאַרמאַכן צו באַגינען?
אין ראָזיקן אונטערוועש, האָט ציטערדיק די רויז געוואַרט,
ס׳זאָלן זיך צודעקן די בלעטעלעך די גרינע.

פאַרבראָכן איז באַ איר געוועזן דאָך דער קאָפּ.
ווי אין די צויבער־נעכט, ווען ס׳זינגט דער סאָלאָוויי איר.
ווען אַף איר שטענגעלע זי שטייט און קוקט אַראָפּ
אונטער דעם שוימיקן לעוואָנעדיקן ווייער.

— כ׳בין ניט קיין סאָלאָוויי: דיר אומקערן איך קאָן דעם טוי.
דיך צוטוליען צום מויל. וועסט עפּשער ווידער אַ צעבלי טאָן?
ביז וויטאָק דיך אָן אָטעם טאָן — אַזוי...
און... בלוט אַ שפּריץ געגעבן האָט פון מיַינע ליפּן...

AT THE BEACH

A solitary figure, alone, at the very edge,
Sits upon the beach, like a statue—motionless,
A sailor with bronzed body. —He has but one arm,
He gazes at the waves breaking at his feet.

To the beach he comes when nobody is there,
Using his teeth, he takes off his jacket
And does not hasten to put it on again,
Even when blisters start forming on his body.

He scans the whole expanse, he measures it,
Between his eyes—drops of perspiration cluster;
The city of Odessa he sees floating in the sea,
Sevastopol he sees reflected in the sea.

Only one arm the war had left him,
And his beloved left only one wound;
It was here he once would walk along with her,
Measuring their steps, like drumsticks in a bowl.

His muscles—they tighten up with longing
Right up to where the arm is severed at the shoulder;
It's sewn together well with skillful stitches,
Yet never can his heart's wound grow together . . .

—If he but could, —his eyes fill up with tears, —
He would then take up the whole blue sea
Like a bard his lute and press it to his breast,
And play out his grief upon its strings.

Secluded, with his shadow—the two together,
Day in, day out to the beach he comes, —
Sits down upon the beach, with his one arm
And, like a statue looks out into the distance—motionless.

באַם פּליאַזש

אַן אָפּגעזונדערטער, אַליין, באַם סאַמע ראַנד,
אָפּן פּליאַזש זיצט, ווי אַ סטאַטוע דאָרט — אומבאַוועגלעך
אַ בראָנדזונלײַביקער מאַטראָס. — ער האָט איין האַנט,
ער קוקט ווי כוואַליעס באַ די פיס זײַנע זיך ברעקלען.

ער קומט צום פּליאַזש, ווען קיינער איז ניטאָ,
העלפט מיט די ציין באַפרײַען פון בושלאַט זיך
און טוט צוריק אים אַזוי גיך ניט אָן,
ביז אַף זײַן לײַב נעמען פּוכירעלעך זיך פּלאַצן.

דעם גאַנצן רוים מיט בליק זײַנעם ער מעסט,
צווישן די אויגן — שוויים געדיכטע טראָפּן;
ער זעט אין יאַם די שווימענדיקע שטאָט אָדעס,
ער זעט אין יאַם זיך שפּיגלען סעוואַסטאָפּאָל.

די קריג האָט אים געלאָזט איין האַנט,
די ליבסטע האָט איין וווּנד געלאָזט אים;
אָט דאָ האָט ער שפּאַצירט מיט איר באַנאַנד,
די טריט, ווי פּולקעס אונטער קליאַש, געמאָסטן.

ס'גיבן די מוסקולן פון בענקשאַפט אים אַ גיי
און בלײַבן שטיין באַם אָפּריס פונעם אַקסל;
ס'איז גוט פאַרצערעוועט מיט מײַסטעריש געניי,
אָבער פון האַרץ די וווּנד ווערט ניט פאַרוואַקסן...

— ווען מע זאָל קאָנען, — גיבן זיך אויגן אַ פאַרגוס, —
וואָלט ער דעם גאַנצן יאַם דעם בלויען,
ווי אַ באַיאַן גענומען אַף דער ברוסט
און אויסגעשפּילט אַף אים זײַן טרויער...

איז אָפּגעזונדערט, מיטן שאָטן — זאַלבאַנאַנד,
צום ברעג קומט ער צו גיין טאָג-טעגלעך, —
זעצט אָפּן פּליאַזש אַוועק זיך מיט איין האַנט
און, ווי אַ סטאַטוע ער קוקט אין ווײַטן — אומבאַוועגלעך.

BY THE SEA AT TWILIGHT

To come out from the sea is difficult at twilight,
It's far more tender then, more enticing, milder;
Though tiny lights are already shining in the mountains,
And shorelines are becoming swathed in veils.

Each speck of sound is spreading out so far,
It's lonely call lingers somewhere in the twilight;
And with its warm mouth quietly clinging, —
Don't leave yet, —the sea itself implores.

The sea flames up at the shore's edge. It burns.
The bared bodies grow more dark and secretive;
From afar the night is drawing near to them
With shadowy footsteps, falling from the trees.

Lifting now their heads towards the leaden earth,
To them seems sweet the nest, welcome the bed;
The babbling silks and linens now frolic about,
And breasts are swaying like underwater bells.

When a wave rolls in around them on emerging,
Boisterous hands grab hold of polished pebbles
And then the bathers look so very like
A shining golden herd around a watering hole.

She splashes and cavorts there undisturbed,
Alone she waits to hear the new moon's piping;
To come out from the sea is difficult at twilight,
It's far more tender then, more enticing, milder.

(1948)

פֿאַרנאַכט בײַם יאַם

אַרויסקריכן פֿון יאַם פֿאַרנאַכט איז שווער,
ער איז נאָך צאַרטער דאַן, פֿאַרופֿנדער און מילדער;
כאָטש ס׳צינדן פֿײַערלעך זיך אָן שוין אין די בערג
און ס׳גיבן ראַנדן זיך אין שלייערס אַ פֿאַרהיל דאָרט.

אָט ווײַט צעטראָגט זיך יעדער ברעקל שטים,
וואָס רופֿט און בלײַבט ערגעץ אין דעמער איינזאַם;
און מיטן וואַרעם מויל, זיך צוטוליענדיק שטיל, —
נאָך ניט אַרויסגיין, — בעט דער יאַם אַליין זיך.

ער צינדט זיך בײַ די ראַנדן אָן. ער ברענט.
די הוילע קערפּערס ווערן טונקלער און געהיימער;
די נאַכט צו זיי פֿון ווײַט געענטנט
מיט טריט פֿון שאָטנס, פֿאַלנדע פֿוןביימער.

פֿאַרהויבנדיק די קעפּ צו דעם ערדיקן בלײַ
ווערט אַזוי זיס די נעסט און גלוסטיק דער געלעגער,
ס׳ווערט אַזוי לעבעדיק דער פֿלאַפּלדיקער זײַד און לײַן
און בריסטן וויגן זיך, ווי אונטערוואַסערדיקע גלעקער.

ווען ס׳וואַלגערט דאָרט אַ כוואַליע אום זיי בײַם אַרויס,
כאַפּן זיך טומלדיקע הענט בײַ שטיינדעלעך בײַ גלאַטע
און דעמאָלט זעען די זיך באָדנדיקע אויס,
ווי אויף דעם וואַסער־טרונק אַ גין־גאָלדענע סטאַדע.

זי פֿליעסקעט זיך און שפּילט זיך אומגעשטערט
און אויף פּײַפּעלע פֿון מוילעד נאָר זי וואַרט דאָרט;
אַרויסקריכן פֿון יאַם פֿאַרנאַכט איז שווער,
ער איז נאָך מילדער דאַן, פֿאַרופֿנדער און צאַרטער.

.1948

FOR THE THIRD TIME

—Don't hinder us, rash wind. Nor ask—to where.
The road with its hidden enchantments is winding;
As gaily the motorcar flies along the road, —
The wind—opposing, and the sun—an escort.

However much the eyes can gather in, —is not enough.
The sun gleams from the bared young bodies, as from mirrors;
A mountain prods the sea with its elbows,
And over the mountains clouds are beginning to unroll.

On the clouds—golden castles are revealed
And on the castles beneath the skies—such a blueness.
The head, in a frenzy lurches up towards it,
But from heat the eyes soon shut, unsatisfied:

—What is there still? Surely something is still there.
There is no end to thirst, nor to the sky;
It barrels along—loaded up to the brim—
So buoyant and youthful, like a joyous song.

Hacked-off calls, swallowed by the wind,
And hands, flapping in the airy-blue transparency;
The motorcar is speeding—hurrying, as if to a wedding,
Tearing through traffic, like a whirlwind.

With a glance into the abyss below, veering and honking,
If going the other way another tries to pass us;
And if like a wave a klaxon should strike the ear,
Then a host of fluttering kerchiefs will wave a greeting

—For the third time we arrive up here at dawn,
For the third time to the green waters of the Riza, —
But it's not enough. Once more—next year
Let our footsteps bring us all back here again.

דאָס דריטע מאָל

— פֿאַרהאַלט ניט, ליַיכטזיניקער ווינט. וווּהין — ניט פֿרעג.
דער וועג מיט קישעף מיט פֿאַרבאָרגענעם זיך דרייט דאָ;
ס׳טראָגט מיט געיובל די מאַשין זיך דורכן וועג, —
דער ווינט — אַנטקעגן און די זון איז אַ באַגלייטער.

וויפֿל די אויגן ניט פֿאַרשעפּן דאָ, — איז קאַרג.
עס ברענט די זון אַף הוילע ליַיבער, גליַיך ווי שפּיגלען;
ס׳שטופּט מיט די עלנבויגנס אָפּ דעם יאַם אַ באַרג,
איבער דעם באַרג פֿון ערגעץ וואָלקנס זיך צעוויקלען.

אַף וואָלקנס — שלעסער דעקן גאָלדענע זיך אָפּ
און אַף די שלעסער אונטער הימלען — אַזאַ בלויקייט.
ס׳גיט זיך אין פֿיבער אַ פֿאַרייַס אַהין דער קאָפּ,
מיט היץ צעשפּאַרן ניט-געזעטיקט זיך די אויגן:

— וואָס איז דאָרט נאָך? עפּעס איז נאָך דאָרטן פֿאַראַן.
ס׳ענדיקט דער דאָרשט זיך ניט אינערגעץ, ווי דער הימל;
ער שפּאַרט אַדורך זיך — אָנגעהויפּנט ביזן ראַנד —
אַזאַ מין אויפֿגאַנגדיקער, יונגער, ווי אַ הימן.

געהאַקטע אויסרופֿן, פֿאַרשלונגענע פֿון ווינט,
און הענט, צעפּאָכעט אין דעם לופֿטיק-בלויען דורכזיכט;
ס׳יאָגט די מאַשין, ווי אַף אַ כאַסענע — געשווינד,
באַ די פֿאַרקערן, ווי אַ וויכער רייַסט זי דורך זיך

מיט בליק אין אָפּגרונט, מיט געדרוי און מיט געפּיַיף,
ס׳זאָל זיך אַ צווייטע פֿון אַנטקעגן מעלדן גיכער;
און אַ געהילך שלאָגט ווי אַ כוואַליע אָן זיך שטיַיף,
עס פֿלאַטערט דורך אַ מענגע גריסנדיקע טיכלעך:

— דאָס דריטע מאָל מיר שטיַיגן אויף דאָ אין קאַיאָר,
דאָס דריטע מאָל צום גרינעם וואַסער פֿון דער ריצאַ, —
אָבער ס׳איז ווייניק. נאָך אַמאָל — איבעראַיאָר
דאָ זאָלן טרעפֿן פֿונדאַסנײַ אונדזערע טריט זיך.

THE GIRL WITH THE BRAIDS

She was so lithe, as she came forward,
Head held high—as if she grew in walking;
Her windblown hair—it seemed was boiling over
And streaming from her head onto her shoulders.

One felt that every moment she grew taller
And let herself be swayed by every breeze;
Her light dress chattered, as if being fanned,
And laughingly her braids cascaded to her hips

And then they were stopped by the sheen of naked legs
That brushed against them, marblelike, opaque,
As if they had leaped out of the foaming stream
With a concealing, shaded, quiet flutter,

And hid themselves, with a rustling at the ends,
Then in repose, the braided strands somehow came undone;
And when the wind rolled one braid over on her breast,
Proudly she tossed it back over her shoulder.

But soon those tresses changed their color to blonde,
When the sun set on them, combed them with a comb of gold;
Lightly and flittingly she walked. Scarcely touching the earth,
Like a young chamois walking on a snow covered mountaintop.

In flames, the setting sun went down,
While she arose . . . and then slowly disappeared . . .
I did not even see her face,
Nor did I think the wonder of it held something more.

דאָס מיידל מיט די צעפּ

אַ בויגיקע, איז זי געגאַן פאָרויס,
דעם קאָפּ — אַרויף, ווי זי וואָלט גייענדיק, געוואַקסן ;
די שוימענדיקע האָר, האָבן געדוכט זיך — זידן אוים
און גיסן זיך פון קאָפּ אַריבער אַף די אַקסל.

ס׳האָט זיך געדוכט, אַז העכער יעדער ווײַל זי ווערט
און לאָזט פון לײַכטסטן ווינטל זיך אַ וויג טאָן ;
געפלאַפּלט האָט דאָס לײַכטע קלייד, ווי אין געפּעכט,
מיט אַ געלעכטער, האָבן צעפּ געפלאָסן ביז די היפטן

און זיך פאַרהאַלטן באַ דעם גלאַנץ פון די אַנטבלויזטע פים,
וואָס האָט געשפּאַרט אַנטקעגן זיי, אַ מירמלנער, אַ מאַטער,
ווי אָפּגעשפּרונגען וואָלטן זיי אינמיטן שוימיקן געפלים
מיט אַ פאַרבאָרגן־שאָטנדיקן, שטילן פלאַטער,

און זיך פאַרטײַעט, שאָרכענדיק באַם שלום,
זיי האָבן נאָכגעלאָזט, ערגעץ צעפלאָכטן אין דער ברייט זיך ;
ווען ס׳האָט דער ווינט איבערגעקויקלט איינעם אַף דער ברוסט,
האָט זי מיט שטאָלץ אַ וואָרף געטאָן צוריק אים אַף דער פלייצע.

געמינעט האָבן זיי זיך, בלאָנדע, אין קאָליר,
די זון האָט זיך אַף זיי געזעצט. מיט קאָם מיט גאָלדענעם
געקעמט זיי ;
זי איז געגאַנגען לײַכט און פלאַטערדיק. די ערד קוים אַ באַריר,
ווי ס׳גייט איבערן שניי פון שפּיצן בערג אַ יונגע געמזע.

אַראָפּגענידערט האָט דער זון־פאַרגאַנג אין ברען,
נאָר זי איז אויפגעגאַן... און ביסלעכווײַז פאַרשוווּנדן...
איך האָב איר פּאָנעם ניט געזען,
כ׳האָב ניט געדענקט, אַז עפּעס נאָך טראָגט אָט דער ווונדער...

UNEXPECTED DIRECTION

If I had noticed then on the station platform
The hand that shows the train's dizzying directions,
And if on one blonde head—a bright blue ribbon
Had caught my eye—would I have gone anywhere at all?

A blue ribbon on a bundle of gold hair,
It dived and reeled above the heads of passengers;
In which direction I should go—suddenly was clear to me,
There was no other, that would not lead me astray.

As sure as the morning comes, surely she is my fate.
On the station. Unexpected yet exactly here.
And I caught a glimpse of golden-brown uncovered legs,
In the shine of a blonde head and the dizzying blue flutter.

די אומגעריכטע ריכטונג

האָב איך באַמערקן דען געקאַנט אפן פּעראָן די האַנט,
וואָס ווײַזט פון צוג די שווינדלדיקע ריכטונג,
און פון אַ בלאָנדן קאָפּ — אַ בלויער באַנט
האָט מיר פאַרשלייפט דעם בליק — אינערגעץ זיך קיין ריר טאָן?

אַ בלויער באַנט אַרום אַ סטויגל בלאָנדע האָר,
ס'האָט זיך געטוקט, געשווינדלט איבער קעפּ פון פּאַסאַזשירן;
אַ וועלכע ריכטונג איך באַדאַרף — איז מיר שוין קלאָר,
קיין אַנדערע איז ניט פאַראַן און וועט אינערגעץ ניט פאַרפירן.

ווי דער פרימאָרגן איז זי מיר באַשערט, געוויס.
אַפּן פּעראָן. אַן אומגעריכטע אַקוראַט דאַ.
און כ'האָב דערזען דעם גלאַנץ פון ברוינע אָפּגעדעקטע פּיס
אין בלאָנדן קאָפּ און אינעם שווינדלדיקן בלויען פלאַטער.

ON A PLATFORM

In the window of the train your head is framed,
You're gazing out with such sad pain of parting;
Night falls. The train wrenches from the platform.
Like the bottom of a depleted sea, all's still and empty . . .

Yet from the rearmost car they do not vanish,
Those tiny crimson lights, wrapped in soft twilight,
Your olive eyes, turning to me now—
Such eyes, so meaningful, so frightened, and so mild . . .

Why does parting seem so much like pain?
Why is it so sweet, that longing from a distance?
Often will I see your eyes still in the glow
Of tiny vanishing fires, hidden in twilight . . .

(1948)

אַפן פעראָן

אין פענצטער פון וואַגאָן איז איַינגערעמט דייַן קאָפּ,
דו קוקסט אַרויס מיט אַזאַ אומעט פון צעשיידונג;
ס׳פאַלט צו די נאַכט. דער צוג רייַסט פון פעראָן זיך אָפּ.
ווי אַף אַ דנאָ פון אויסגעשעפּטן יאַם ווערט שטיל און ליידיק...

נאָר עס פאַרשווינדן ניט פון הינטערשטן וואַגאָן
די רויטע פייַערלעך אין ווייכער דעמערונג פאַרהילטע,
ווי דייַנע איילבירט־אויגן, וואָס זיי קערן מיר איצט אָן —
אַזעלכע ניט־דערזאָגטע און דערשראָקענע, און מילדע...

פאַרוואָס דערנעענטערט די צעשיידונג ביז צו פייַן?
פאַרוואָס איז אַזוי זיס די בענקשאַפט פון דער ווייַטן?
כ׳וועל דייַנע אויגן זען אַ לאַנגע צייַט נאָך אין דער שייַן
פון די פאַרשווינדנדיקע פייַערלעך אין דעמערונג פאַרטייַטע...

.1948

YOUR GLANCE

From every journey into wishful dreams
I soon return—in height a little shorter;
Your glance, so innocent, it lets me know,
That the taller me you see is but your fancy.

Yet such a radiance dwells within your glance,
It keeps my head from bowing down with guilt,
Even when in my heart remorse should blossom,
Even when tears should sparkle in my eyes . . .

In these spectral pursuits, so fanciful,
The way to you grows clearer and draws closer,
And, casting my heart over distances to you,
I let myself be singed, wherever there's a flame.

(1948)

דײַן בליק

פֿון יעדער רײַזע אין דעם אויסגעדוכטן גליק
קער איך זיך אום — אין וווּקס אַ ביסל קורצער;
מיר גיט צװױסן עס דײַן אומשולדיקער בליק,
וואָס מיט אַמאָל אַזאַ מין הויכער מיר ער דוכט זיך...

נאָר אַזאַ שטראַלנדיקס פֿאַראַן איז אין דײַן בליק,
וואָס לאָזט דעם קאָפּ מײַנעם אין שולד זיך דאָך ניט בויגן,
אַפֿילו ווען אין האַרץ כאַראַפּטע זיך צעבליט
און ווען אַ טרער פֿאַרבלישטשעט אין די אויגן...

אױף די געיעגן געשפּענטיקס, נאָך געדאַכטס,
ווערט מיר דער וועג צו דיר געלײַטערטער און נעענטער,
און, איבערוואַרפֿנדיק אױף שטרעקעס דיר מײַן האַרץ,
לאָז איך זיך דאָך, אױף ווי אַ פֿײַערל, אַ ברען טאָן.

.1948

BY THE SEA

Are you returning now in the sunset's flame—
The last of those, who having bathed, seek rest;
The molten sea, it's calmly watching you
With all its clamoring gold-threaded splashes.

You should let them sprinkle over you
So that they reflect the sheen of your browned skin:
The sea, it's stretching out, rising toward the sky
And golden featherbeds are everywhere unrolling upon it.

To the sea, you surely do not seem too small,
Compared with its all-overflowing wave,
When you are bending down to bare your feet,
When you're shaking the pebbles from a sandal that has come off.

Or when, in disarray, your dripping wet hair
Tumbles heavily down in all its dark luster,
Revealing a bit of shoulder and a neck,
Glowing like burnished amber in the sun's last rays.

To the sea, you do not seem too small in your haste.
It sees you rising. It sees that it has enticed you.
It sees you turning back toward it for the moment,
With a dreamy look of still expectant longing.

At last, it takes upon itself the entire sunset,
And everywhere there's light so that it can marvel—
How with your naked feet you talk to the polished pebbles
And how they answer you with their noisy scattering.

Now in its flaming it needs solemnity,
It needs to achieve a certain grandeur now;
Yet, when it looks up at you, the sea grabs hold of heaven,
Like a child who catches hold of its mother's dress.

באָם יאַם

קערסט עפּשער אום זיך איצט אינעם פֿאַרגייענדיקן פּלאַם —
די לעצטע צווישן די, וואָס גייען, אויסגעבאָדענע, אַף רו שוין,
און ס׳קוקט דיר נאָך, אינגאַנצן אַ צעשמאָלצענער, דער יאַם
מיט זײַנע רוישנדיקע גאָלד־געוועבטע פּליושן.

דו זאָלסט פֿון ווײַט זיי טאָן אַף זיך אַ כאַפּ אַרויף
און לאָזן זיי אין דײַן פֿאַרברוין זיך טאָן אַ שפּיגל:
ער ציט זיך אוים, דער יאַם, ער הייבט זיך ביזן הימל אויף
און איבערבעטן גאָלדענע אַף אים זיך געבן אַ צעוויקל.

דו דוכסט זיך אים ניט אוים צו קליין, געוויס,
אינעם פֿאַרגלײַך מיט זײַן דורכויס פֿאַרפּלייצנדיקער כוואַליע,
ווען בויגסט זיך אָן, אַנטבלויזנדיק די פֿיס,
ווען טרייסלסט אוים אַ שטיינדעלע פֿון אַן אַראָפּגעפֿאַלענער
סאַנדאַליע,

ווען ס׳גיבן אין אומאָרדענונג אַ שווערן פֿאַל
מיט שוואַרצן גלאַנין די האָר דײַנע די אויסגענעצטע
און דעקן אָפּ אַ שטיקל אַקסל און דעם האַלדז,
ווי אָנגעשליפֿענעם בורשטין אין שטראַלן לעצטע.

דו דוכסט זיך אים ניט אוים צו קליין אין דײַן געאײַל,
ער זעט, ווי הייבסט זיך אויף. ער זעט, ווי לאָזט זיך אַ פֿאַרנאַר טאָן,
ער זעט, ווי דרייסט זיך אוים צו אים נאָך אַף אַ ווײַל
מיט אַ פֿאַרטרוימטן בליק אַ ניטגעזעטיקטן פֿון וואַרטן.

און נעמט אַף זיך דעם גאַנצן זונפֿאַרגאַנג צו לעצט,
ס׳זאָל ליכטיק זײַן דעם רוים זיך איבעראַשן —
ווי מיט די הוילע פֿיס צו די געטאַקטע שטיינדעלעך דו רעדסט
און ווי זיי ענטפֿערן דיר אָפּ, צעשיטנדיק זיך, ראַשיק...

מ׳דאַרף איצט אַ פֿײַערלעכקייט זײַן אין זײַן געפּלאַם,
ער דאַרף אַ גרויסער זײַן אַצינד אַזאַ מין;
דאָך, קוקנדיק אַף דיר, כאַפּט ער באַם הימל זיך, דער יאַם,
ווי ס׳כאַפּט אַ קינד זיך באַ דער פּאָלע פֿון דער מאַמען.

INSIDE AND OUT

The day grows ever shorter. The sky is lowering.
The sun has set, reminding us that time has passed;
I walk around inside you still, as in a forest,
Where—inside and out—everything's tangled, bewitched.

Your heart is beside me. I hear it like a running spring,
From inside itself, yet I know not how to reach it;
I walk around inside you still, as in a forest,
A place where I have never been before . . .

The shadows greet each other. They try to bar the way.
They erase the road, so that no one can see it;
I walk inside you still, as in a forest,
And the more I walk, the more I go astray . . .

I keep you in my heart, away from every eye,
Not seeing how myself I bar the way to you;
I walk inside you still, as in a forest,
And every moment I'm quickening my footsteps.

The day is waning. It will be over soon . . .
So what if it's over? If it's night? If it's dark?
I walk around inside you still, as in a forest,
And, just as the first time, I tread a path from inside myself to you.

אײַן און אויס

דער טאָג ווערט קלענער וואָס אַמאָל. דער הימל פּאַלט.
די זון פֿאַרגייט און זי דערמאָנט, אַז ס'איז ניט פֿרי שוין;
איך גיין נאָך אַלץ אין דיר אַרום, ווי אין אַ וואַלד,
ווו — אײַן און אויס — פֿאַרפּלאָנטערט איז, פֿאַרקישעפֿט.

דערנעבן איז דײַן האַרץ. איך הער עס, ווי אַ קוואַל
פֿון זיך אַליין, נאָר כ'ווייס ניט ווי אַזוי צו אים גענענען;
איך גיין נאָך אַלץ אין דיר אַרום, ווי אין אַ וואַלד,
ווו איך בין קיינמאָל ניט געווען נאָך...

די שאָטנס גריסן זיך. עס גיט מיך יעדער אַ פֿאַרהאַלט
דעם וועג פֿאַרשטרײַכן זיי. דער וועג זאָל זיך ניט אָנזען;
איך גיי נאָך אַלץ אין דיר אַרום, ווי אין אַ וואַלד,
וואָס מער איך גיי, אַלץ מער איך בלאָנדזשע...

פֿון יעדנס אויג אין האַרץ דײַך איך האַלט
און זע ניט, ווי מיט זיך אַליין דעם וועג צו דיר פֿאַרשטעל איך,
איך גיי נאָך אַלץ אין דיר אַרום, ווי אין אַ וואַלד,
און יעדן אויגנבליק די טריט מײַנע כ'פֿאַרשנעלער.

דער טאָג פֿאַרגייט. דער טאָג איז אויס שוין באַלד...
איז וואָס, אַז אויס? איז וואָס, אַז נאַכט? איז וואָס, אַז כווישעך?
איך גיי נאָך אַלץ אין דיר אַרום, ווי אין אַ וואַלד,
און טרעט, ווי ס'ערשטע מאָל, אַ שטעגל צו דיר אויס זיך.

YOUR TEAR

Your glance is branded into me. It silences me.
And it forces me to bow my head down low,
When, as from a fever, your face begins to twitch,
When in your eyes a trembling tear appears.

Swollen and full to dripping, it looks at me,
Then with a little shake it splashes down;
No image of me do I see in it, only my guilt.
It does not make demands, but only drowns its grievance in itself.

Nor does it hasten to detach itself
From your eyelashes but lingers there, quivering and twitching;
The world in it becomes two times as large
And in it the pupils of your eyes only grow larger.

(1948)

דײַן טרער

ער מאַכט מיך שטיל, דײַן בליק. געשמידט אין זיך.
און גיט צו דר'ערד דעם קאָפּ מײַנעם אַ בויג אָן,
ווען ס'פּיבערט דורך אַ צוק אַף דײַן געזיכט,
ווען ס'ציטערט אויף אַ טרער אין דײַנע אויגן.

מיט אָנגעקוואָלנקייט זי גלאַנצט, אַז אָנגעטריפטע פול,
אָט גיט זי זיך אַ פליוכנדיקן וויג אַריבער;
מײַן אָפּבילד זע איך ניט אין איר, איך זע מײַן שולד.
נאָר ניט זי מאָנט, אַליין אין זיך דערטרינקט זי דעם פאַריבל.

און ניט זי רײַסט פון דײַנע וויִעם זיך אַרויס,
פאַרצוקט זי בלײַבט אין דײַנע וויִעם צאַפּלען;
די וועלט אין איר ווערט נאָך אַמאָל אַזוי די גרויס
און ס'גיבן זיך אין איר נאָר אַ פאַרגרעסער די שוואַרצאַפּלען...

.1948

BY A RIVER

Having bathed, they came out from the river—
As from a chase—bronzed, glistening, and young.
And loudly, laughingly, they leaped into the air as one;
And shaking off the water, they went cavorting.

With such abandon, as if they were dancing
Together with the ringing, joy-filled summer;
Wearing upon each one's head—a wreath of sea-grass
And the fragrant sun no longer bakes them any darker.

All by themselves the little braids came loose.
All by themselves the knees, gave way, in jest—
They laze around together on the grass
With their backs exposed, and with their feet in the water.

Four little girlish heads, caressed by the river,
Were perched upon eight youthful shoulders—
The moments weigh upon them so very lightly,
As they let their feet keep dipping in the river.

As if they meant to hold it with their feet,
That it should not go away, so they could keep it near.—
And from time to time one hears a burst of laughter.
And from time to time they try to keep away the sun.

—Your laughter, girls, is fresher than the river.
It's a joy to let oneself be swallowed by its waves:
There's no one else but you that I belong with,
Bronzed from the sun, laughing, glistening, and young.

(1948)

באַם טײַך

זײ זײַנען אויסגעבאָדענע אַרום פֿון טײַך —
װי פֿון געיעג — פֿאַרברױנטע, גלאַנציקע און יונגע.
און הילכיק, לאַכנדיק, אַ שפּרונג געטאָן באַגלײַך.
און אָפּטרײסלען דאָס װאַסער זיך געלאָזט אין די געשפּרונגען.

װי אָפּגעלאָזט אַזױ מע װאָלט זיך אין אַ טאַנץ
מיט דעם באַגליקנדיקן גלעקלדיקן זומער;
באַ יעדן אַפֿן קאָפּ — פֿון װאַסער־גראָז אַ קראַנץ
און שמעקעדיקע זון שטײט צום פֿאַרברױן ניט צו מער.

אַלײן האָבן די צעפּלעך זיך געגעבן אַ צעלאָז.
אַלײן האָבן די קני אַ בױג געטאָן מיט שפּאַס זיך. —
אָט ליגט מען שױן צעװאַלגערט אַפֿן גראָז
מיט רוקנדלעך — אַרױף און מיט די פֿיס אין װאַסער.

פֿיר קעפּלעך מײדלשע, פֿאַרצערטלטע פֿון טײַך
אױף יונגע אַקסלעך אױף אַכט אַרױפֿגעזעצטע. —
זײ טראָגן יעדער װײַלע אױף זיך אַזױ לײַכט,
לאָזן די פֿיס זיך יעדער װײַל אין טײַך אַ נעץ טאָן.

װי צוגעהאַלטן װאָלטן זײ אַזױ אים מיט די פֿיס,
אַז ניט אַװעק ער זאָל, זײ זאָלן האָבן אים דערנעבן. —
און אַלע װײַל גיט אַ געלעכטער זיך אַ רים.
און אַלע װײַל אַ טרײַב די זון פֿון זיך זײ געבן.

— אײַער געלעכטער, מײדלעך, פֿרישער איז פֿון טײַך.
פֿון זײַנע כװאַליעס איז אַ פֿרײד צו לאָזן זיך פֿאַרשלונגען:
איך קער מיט קײנעם זיך ניט אָן אַזױ אָ, װי מיט אײַך,
פֿאַרברױנטע, לאַכנדיקע, גלאַנציקע און יונגע.

.1948

IN THE RAIN

1

No shore awaits us anywhere,
Nor anywhere do the roads wait for us;
The two of us are swimming through the night
Under an early *Khezhvn*[16] rain.

The dark of night—upon us, so that we see nothing,
And beneath us—the river, the depths, and our youth.
Only in our eyes—the fatedness and fervor
Of two trains that run in opposite directions.

The darkness reminds us of those distances,
That neither one of us can ever measure, —
Only the echo of our heartbeats seems so near,
The river will soon burst into loud applause . . .

From up above, a lash of light has touched us,
A star above us is rolling like a wheel, —
Today it shall be ours, the rolling star,
Like a sea gull, with our eyes we'll circle round it.

2

It seems to me, that nothing ever happened till today,
It seems to me, that now the world is just beginning;
As if a pair of swords, dipped in radiant light,
Were slashing a wide path across our throats.

At times, a hand would flash out from the river,
Now a white head scarf, now a suntanned shoulder,
And thus, throughout the night we swam, we two together—
By waves—divided, by waves—made into one.

Moonlight-glow, woven from the foam,
It glides, it's calling to the coldest darkness;
—Please wait. Somewhere a tree is reaching towards us,
I do not see it, —I only sense it by the sound . . .

16. A month in autumn.

אונטער אַ רעגן

.1

קיין ברעג אינערגעץ אַף אונדז וואַרט,
ס'וואַרטן אינערגעץ ניט אַף אונדז קיין וועגן;
באַצווייט מיר שווימען דורך דער נאַכט
אונטער אַן אַנהייב-כעשוועשדיקן רעגן.

די גאַנצע נאַכט — אַף אונדז, מיר זאָלן גאָרניט זען,
און אונטער אונדז — דער טײַך, דער אָפּגרונט און די יוגנט;
נאָר אין די בליקן — אומפאַרמײַדלעכקייט און ברען
פון צוויי אַנטקעגן-גייענדיקע צונגן.

אין ווײַטקייטן די פינצטערניש דערמאָנט,
וואָס קיינער צווישן אונדז קאָן ניט קיין מעסט טאָן, —
יאָר דער געהילך פון הערצער הערט זיך אַזוי נאָנט,
דער טײַך וועט באַלד, ווי פון אַן אויפרײַס זיך צעפּליעסקען...

מ'רירט פון דער הויך אונדז אָן אַ בײַטשל שײַן,
אַ שטערן איבער אונדז זיך קײַקלט, ווי אַ רייפל, —
ער וועט הײַנט אונדזערער, דער שטערן זײַן,
מיר וועלן מיט די בליקן ווי אַ מעווע אים פאַרשלייפן.

.2

מיר דאַכט, אַז ס'איז נאָך גאָרנישט ניט געווען ביז הײַנט,
מיר דאַכט, זי הייבט אַצינד ערשט אָן, די וועלט זיך;
זוי שוועדן צוויי, געטונקענע אין שײַן,
זיך פעכטן אַף אַ שטרעקע ווײַט אונדזערע העלדזער.

אַ יעדער ווײַל בליצט אויף פון טײַך אַ האַנט,
אַ קאָפּ-טיכל אַ ווײַס און אַ פאַרברוינטער אַקסל;
אַזוי אַ דורך דער נאַכט מיר שווימען זאַלבאַנאַנד —
דורך כוואַליעס — אָפּגעטיילט, דורך כוואַליעס — אײַנגעוואַקסן...

לעוואָנע-שײַן, געוועבט פון שוים
זיך גליטשט, פאַרופנדיק צום קאַלטסטן כוישעך;
— וואַרט אוים. ערגעץ שטרעקט זיך צו אונדז אַ בוים,
איך זע אים ניט, — איך הער נאָר בלויז לויטן גערויש אים...

—Stretch out your hand to me, be quick.
We'll have a dance under the *Khezhvn* rain.
The wind, it played the role of the best man,
And there proceeding towards us—was the tree . . .

3

Greetings to you, tree, from the rainy night,
Amidst man's unrest and the wind's commotion.
Beneath the shelter of your branching roof,
We'll take our rest now, like Adam and like Eve.

We will not touch your leaves, not a single one,
We've shed our own. We came here lightly clad;
In fall we knocked upon the door to spring,
And opened wide our hearts to it alone.

You have no fruit? So be it. We bring the fruit with us.
Let only a bit of moonlight shine through your leaves.
It will suffice us—to lick from our faces the drops of rain,
And grow drunk on them, as on the sweetest honey.

Who cares if it's fall? So what if leaves are falling?
Can then a rain-sodden tree not be sufficient?
Can then a gush of rain not be enough
To welcome as a guest our wayfaring youth?

4

There's room enough here, beloved, —come inside.
With eyes closed shut one cannot see a star;
Today I do not know how many years I have,
I do not count them, nor do I count the stars in the sky.

I only see them, and—they will always be.
But even a moment can be an eternity;
Oh my constant one, my dear one—come inside,
It's out with time, there's no end and no beginning.

Did not a sliver of moon lie down upon you?
Did not a sliver of its body pierce you? —
But for me it's light, and I can touch the light
With my lips, with my hands, as if it were my most blessed morsel.

צי אוים די הענט צו מיר, געשווינד.
ס'וועט זײַן אַ טאַנץ אין כעשוועדיקן רעגן.
גענומען אונטערפירעכטס האָט דער ווינט
און ס'איז דער בוים געגאַנגען אונדז אַנטקעגן...

.3

זײַ, בוים, באַגריסט מיט רעגנדיקער נאַכט,
מיט אומרו מענטשלעכן און ווינטיקן געהאַווע.
מיר וועלן אונטער דײַן צעצווײַגטן דאַך
זיך אָפּרוען אַצינד, ווי אָדאָם און ווי כאַווע.

מירן צו דײַנע בלעטער זיך ניט טאָן קיין ריר,
די אייגענע אַראָפּגעפּליקט. געקומען לײַכט אַהערצו;
אין האַרבסט אַ קלאַפּ געטאָן צום פרילינג אין דער טיר
און אויפגעשפּאַרט פאַר אים אַליין די הערצער.

האָסט ניט קיין פרוכט? איז ניט. מיר טראָגן פרוכט מיט זיך.
לאָז נאָר דורך בלעטער דורך אַ ביסל שײַן פון דער לעוואָנע.
עס וועט אונדז זײַן גענוג — די טראָפּנס רעגן פון געזיכט
אַראָפּלעקן פאַרשיקערט, ווי דעם זיסטן האָניק.

וואָס איז דען, אַז ס'איז האַרבסט? אַז בלעטער-פאַל, איז וואָס?
איז דען אַ בוים אָן אויסגעגעצטער ניט געגוגנד, —
איז ניט גענוגנד דען אַ רעגנדיקער גאַס
אָף מאַכנעס-אוירעך זײַן די בלאָנדזשענדיקע יוגנט?

.4

ס'איז דאָ געווים, געגאַרטע, — גיי אַרײַן.
מיט צוגעמאַכטע אויגן זעט זיך ניט קיין שטער אָן;
איך ווייס ניט וויפל יאָרן ס'איז מיר הײַנט,
איך צייל זיי ניט, ווי מ'צייל אין הימל ניט די שטערן.

איך זע זיי בלויז און זיי — זיי וועלן שטענדיק זײַן
נאָר אויך אָן אויגנבליק קאָן האָבן דעם באַטרעף פון שטענדיק;
אָ, שטענדיקע, געגאַרטע, — גיי אַרײַן,
ס'איז אוים מיט צײַט, קיין אָנהייב און קיין ענדע.

צי ס'האָט אַ פּאַסיקל לעוואָנע זיך געלייגט אָף דיר,
צי ס'האָט זיך לײַב אַ פּאַסיקל פון דיר אַדורכגעריסן, —
נאָר ס'איז מיר ליכטיק, און דאָס ליכט כ'באַריר
מיט ליפּן, מיט די הענט, ווי מײַן געבענטשסטן ביסן.

I thank you, night and tree, and those suckling branches,
No matter—for how long you have been given to me.
The glistening wet leaves are whispering to each other
And gossiping about me in such a sweet outpouring…

אַ דאַנק דיר, נאַכט און בוים, און צווײַגיקער פֿאַרזויג,
אַלציינגם — אַף וויפֿל ווײַל געשענקט מיר ביסטו.
די גלאַנציק־פֿײַכטע בלעטער שושקען זיך אַזוי
און זיי באַרעדן מיך מיט אַזאַ זים געפֿליסטער...

CAUCASUS

1

A roadway—up, a roadway—down,
Vaults made of stone, like arches;
From up above the snore rolls down,
The snore of sleeping mountain-ness.

Its heart then gives a sudden lurch,
The abyss below is shut for it
And high above those bottomless depths,
The eagles' mansard-roofs are swaying.

2

—A passerby should be allowed
As guest in a mansard for a while.
A drink of water—the dust wiped off, —
A passerby, would he need much?

—I know: to nests of eagles—free,
Only the winds can gather there;
Along the way I'll find a kinsman,
One who will surely know of me.

3

Their heads are craning towards the sky,
Their shoulders stretched to darkening clouds, —
The cliffs are waiting for a call—
And one has grown into another.

They boldly catch a lightning flash,
They let nothing split them apart;
To me it seems: —high up, on the crest
Demons and ghosts have come to pasture.

קאַווקאַז

.1

אַ וועג — אַרויף, אַ וועג — אַראָפּ,
געוועלבן שטיינערנע, ווי אַרקעס;
פון דר׳הויך דערקײַקלט זיך דער כראָפּ,
דער כראָפּ פון שלאָפנדיקער באַרג-קייט.

ער גיט אין האַרץ זיך אַ פאַרטריף,
די אָפּגרונט-טיף פאַר אים צעשפּאַרט איז
און איבער אָפּגרונטיקער טיף
זיך וויגן אָדלערשע מאַנסאַרדעס.

.2

— זאָל זײַן אַ דורכגייער דערלויבט
אַ ווײַל צו גאַסט אין אַ מאַנסאַרדע.
אַ טרונק — און אָפּווישן דעם שטויב, —
באַדאַרף אַ דורכגייער אַ סאַך דען?

איך ווייס: צו אָדלער-נעסטן — פרײַ
בלויז ווינטן זיך דערקלויבן קאָנען;
געפינען כ׳וועל אין וועג אַ פרײַנט,
פון זיי וועט טמעץ מיך דערקאָנען.

.3

די קעפּ פאַריסן אָף אַרוף,
פאַר כמאַרעס אויסגעשטרעקט די אַקסל, —
וואַרטן די פעלדזן אָף אַ רוף —
איינס אין דעם צווייטן אײַנגעוואַקסן.

זיי כאַפּן איבער דרײַסט אַ בליץ,
זיי לאָזן זיך ניט קיין צערײַס טאָן;
מיר דוכט: — אינדר׳הויך, אָף זייער שפּיץ
זיך פּאַשען דעמאָנעס און גײַסטער.

4

So it seems to me. And—if not,
Perhaps I brought them here myself,
From fairy tales that are preserved
In both my heart and memory. —

Now I call them forth in sound.
What more do I need on such a day?
I will not linger here too long,
But only pass through like a shadow.

5

Over there a giant threatens—huge,
There from a mountain a horn blares forth.
There a rushing river whips by,
And among the scattered stones is lost.

One cliff is pressed against another,
A third one grabs them by their necks;
—Welcoming, Caucasus, is your threshold
To stillness, just as to a tempest.

6

A sound follows the path—hiding
In its stony cage, as if conspiring;
But it soon grows clear: —a mountain stream
Now lets itself be heard from afar.

And then it sparkles up with foam,
It seems to spring from mountain caves;
For once again it disappears,
We only hear it telling tales.

7

"With golden axes cleaves the sun
—The mountains' hoary heads of ice;
The ice-forged citadel then falls
And whatever falls is rent apart."

.4

אַזוי מיר דוכט. און — טאָמער ניט,
האָב איך מיט זיך אַהער געבראַכט זיי.
פון באַבע־מײַסעס אויסגעהיט,
אינעם זיקאָרן און אין האַרצן. —

איך רוף זיי אויף אַצינד אין קלאַנג.
וואָס דאַרף איך נאָך אין אַזאַ אַ טאָג ?
פאַרהאַלטן כ'וועל זיך דאָ ניט לאַנג,
אַדורכגיין בלויז כ'וועל ווי אַ שאָטן.

.5

דאָ דראָט אַ ריז — פאַרמאָסטן — גלײַך,
דאָ פון אַ באַרג זיך רײַסט אַ האָרן.
דאָ טראָגט זיך, שמײַסנדיק, אַ טײַך
צווישן געוואַלגער־שטיין פאַרלאָרן.

דאָ דריקט אַ פעלדז אַ צווייטן פעלדז,
דאָ אָפן קאַרק זיי נעמט אַ דריטער ;
— ס'איז גאַסטפרײַנטלעך, קאַווקאַז, דײַן שוועל
פאַר שטילקייט גלײַך, ווי פאַר געוויטער.

.6

דעם וועג באַגלייט אַ רויש — פאַרטײַט
אין שטיינער־שטײַג, ווי אַ פאַרשווערונג ;
נאָר באַלד ווערט קלאָר : — אַ באַרגנטײַך
לאָזט וועגן זיך פון ווײַט צו הערן.

דערנאָך גיט ער אַ גלאַנץ מיט שוים,
עס דוכט — ער שפּרינגט פון באַרג דורך היילן ;
און ווידער זעט מען אים ניט שוין,
מע הערט אים עפּעס נאָר דערציילן.

.7

„— מיט העק מיט גאָלדענע דאָרט שפּאַלט
די זון באַ בערג די גרויע אײַז־קעפּ ;
די אײַז־געשמידטע פעסטונג פאַלט
און דאָס געפאַלענע צערײַסט זיך."

—Let it be so. I hear and—don't hear.
Although the river's howl resounds;
And in its course it bears along
My reflection with it to the sea.

8

The riverbed is filled with pebbles,
The river clings to it, like green moss;
And each of them pursues the other,
Stirring up a foaming torrent.

Like a tribute to the sea—the mountains,
Bear tufts of clouds upon their heads,
And imperceptibly they change,
From one moment to the next.

9

It's soon too crowded at the bottom,
One riverbed is too narrow for them;
They need more room, and then some more.
They count themselves, as at a dinner.

Soon others join them on the way,
They turn the ice into a spring;
They rush about at break-neck speed
Churning and roaring all the while.

10

Somewhere they chew up a mountain,
Somewhere they saw off a cliff;
They leap about in swirling loops,
Like the rounded arcs of rainbows.

They attack the stone with a fury,
And fight each other to break free,
Then – one more surge, one more rockface,
And then they're torn apart in two's.

— זאָל זײַן אַזוי. איך הער און — ניט.
כאַטש דער געוואָי פון טײַך זיך צאַפּלט;
און טראַגנדיק זיך, שלעפּט ער מיט
אין יאָם אַרײַן מיט זיך מײַן אָפּבילד.

.8

געבעט מיט שטיינער איז זײַן דנאָ,
דער שטראָם אים שאָבט, ווי גרינע ליסקע;
און איינער יאָגט דעם צווייטן נאָך
מיט אַ צעשוימיקטן געפּליסטער.

ווי צינש דעם יאָם — געשיקט פון בערג, —
אַף קעפּ זיי טראָגן שטיקער כמאַרע
און בײַטן פּליסיק, אומבאַמערקט,
אַ יעדער ווײַל אין וועג די מאַרע.

.9

אַש ווערט זיי ענג שוין אַפן דנאָ,
אָט ווערט שוין אין איין פּלוס-בעט שמאָל זיי;
זיי דאַרפן מער, זיי דאַרפן נאָך.
זיי ציילן זיך, ווי אַף אַ מאָלצײַט.

אָט שטייען צו אין וועג שוין נאָך,
מיט אײַז זיי לאָזן זיך אַ קוואָל טאָן;
אָט טראָגן זיי זיך שוין מיט בראָך
און מיט געברום און מיט געוואַלגער.

.10

ערגעץ צעפּרעסן זיי אַ בארג,
אַ פעלדז זיי זעגן ערגעץ אונטער
און שפּרינגען אום צעשוימיקט-רונד,
ווי האַלבע רעגנבויגנס רונדע.

און מאָרדעווען דעם שטיין מיט האַסט,
און שלאָגן זיך פּאַר וועלן פרײַ זײַן;
אָט — נאָך אַ וואַלגער, נאָך אַ פּלאַסט,
און זיך אַף צווייען זיי צערײַסן.

11

Now two are flowing—up and down,
As if upon a rocky ladder;
It seems as if, when one flows down,
The other rushes back up again.

Both at once then disappear,
Only noise remains—muffled—grating;
The mountain stream still flows somewhere,
And lets itself be heard from afar.

12

Here, within the realm of splendor,
In the shadow of the palm leaves,
I'm reminded of a summer night
Back in Volhynia, in my dead *shtetl*.

By the stream frogs croak—alone,
And the moon is full and bright;
Young and old bring out their bedding,
Making beds to sleep outdoors . . .

13

The breeze from the stream blows on them all,
Their beards, their nightcaps, it caresses;
Somewhere a child begins to cry,
So the whole *shtetl* is awakened.

They sleep, like blades of grass by the wayside,
Like the white goats in Volhynia,
And the river wakes up anew,
With a wail and a shrill tremolo.[17]

14

- For what reason wails the stream? —I hear.
Has it again become too crowded?
For there are corpses in the mountains,
Come from my home to fill my dreams,

17. *fartsikl*: Alludes to a form of cantorial singing.

.11

אָט פליסן צוויי שוין — אויף און אָפּ,
ווי אַף אַ שטיינעריקן לייטער;
עס דוכט, אַז איינער פליסט אַראָפּ
און צריק אינדר׳הויך זיך רײַסט דער צווייטער.

און ביידע זיי פֿאַרשווינדן גלײַך,
און בלויז געדויש — פֿאַרטײַעט — שווערער;
ער לויפֿט ערגעץ, דער באַרגנטײַך,
און לאָזט פון זיך אַף ווײַט צו הערן.

.12

דאָ, אין דעם קעניגרײַך פון פּראַכט,
אין שאָטן פון די פּאַלמען־בלעטער,
דערמאָנט זיך מיר אַ זומער־נאַכט
אין מײַן וואָלינער טויטן שטעטל.

עס קוואָקען פרעש באַם טײַך — אַליין,
ס׳איז די לעוואָנע אַזאַ גרויסע;
מיט בעט־געוואַנט גייט גרוים און קליין
פון שטוב זיך אויסבעטן אינדרויסן...

.13

צו אַלע קומט פון טײַך דער ווינט,
די בערד, די טשיפּיקעס אַ גלעט טאָן;
צעוויינט זיך ערגעץ־ווו אַ קינד,
איז כאַפּט זיך אויף דאָס גאַנצע שטעטל.

זיי שלאָפן, ווי דאָס גראָז באַם וועג,
ווי די וואָלינער ווײַסע ציגן;
און ס׳גיט אַפּסנײַ דער טײַך אַ וועק,
זיך אַ צעוואָי און אַ פֿאַרציקל...

.14

— וואָס וויל דער וואָי פון טײַך? — איך הער.
שוין ווידער ענג איז מיט אַמאָל אים?
עס זײַנען מייסים אין די בערג
פון דר׳היים געקומען מיר צו כאָלעם.

I'll say the mourning prayers for them,
I'll not forget them on my way;
Grass—from beneath, snow—from above,
And cliff with forest—witnesses.[18]

15

A beehive on a field of green,
Unexpectedly appears,
When a hundred-year-old man,
Tall as a mountain—and hoary, —

Bowing, greets them, one and all,
Interrupts my recollections:
—Passers-by, d'you want a drink? —
And points to a spring nearby, so lovely . . .

16

Peace dwells in his ancient look,
And a blessing—in his sage-like gesture;
Bees are flying to and fro,
Bringing him delight from the mountains.

Each blade of grass—in sweetness revels,
The sun on every leaflet quivers;
—Welcoming, Caucasus, is your threshold
To stillness, just as to a tempest.

17

Refreshing is a drink from the mountains,
The water has soaked up their power;
They stretch up high their verdant beards,
Standing fast on naked paws.

And it seems that this old fellow,
Is not just master of the bees;
Over mountains too he spreads his hand,
They too are his obedient servants.

18. *vekslen* (sing. *veksl*): Promissory notes.

כ׳זאָל טרויער אָפּריכטן נאָך זיי,
כ׳זאָל ניט פאַרגעסן אונטערוועג זיי;
פון אונטן — גראָז, פון אויבן — שניי
און פעלדז מיט וואַלד זיך צווישן — וועקסלען.

.15

אַ בינשטאָק אַף אַ גרינעם לאָן
גיט אומגעריכט דאָרט אַ באַווייַז זיך,
אַ הונדערטיערעדיקער מאַן,
גלייַך ווי אַ באַרגנהויך — אַ גרייַזער, —

ער גריסט מיט אַ פאַרנויג זיך רונד,
רייַסט די דערמאָנונגען מיר איבער:
— צי וויל דער דורכגייער אַ טרונק? —
ווייַזט אַף אַ קוואַל, דערנעבן, ליבער...

.16

ס׳איז פרידן אין זייַן אַלטן בליק
און בראָכע — אין זייַן קלוגער מי איז;
די בינען פליִען הין און צריק,
פון בערג זיי ליפערן אים כיִעס.

אַ יעדער גראָז — מיט זיסקייט קוועלט,
די זון אַף יעדער בלעטל ציטערט;
— ס׳איז גאַסטפרייַנטלעך, קאַווקאַז, דייַן שוועל
פאַר שטילקייט גלייַך, ווי פאַר געוויטער.

.17

דערקוויַקנד איז דער טרונק פון בערג,
מיט קראַפט פון זיי דאָס וואַסער זאַט איז;
זיי שטרעקן הויך די גרינע בערד
און שטייען פעסט אַף הוילע פיאַטעס.

און ס׳דוכט, אַז אָט דער אַלטער מאַן
איז ווירט ניט נאָר איבער די בינען,
נאָר אויך אַף בערג זיך שפרייט זייַן האַנט,
אויך זיי געהאָרכזאַם אים באַדינען.

18

He seems to fit in here so well
Among all the mighty growths;
From sad remembrances he frees me
But sends them back to me too soon.

I look at him in silent wonder,
As on unfathomable beauty;
Pleasant is his voice to me,
Though I don't understand his language.

19

Each mountain is a home to him
And every tree for him a tent,
And in his wrinkles I can read
The harshness of these rugged places.

Yet his health seems none the worse,
He wields a power over time;
Either it's the sun he's battling,
Or the flooding of the mountains.

20

Cleverly he struggles. Overcomes them,
But later they become like kin;
And, like a rain that's quickly over,
He too brightens up anew.

Each stream is at his beck and call
And every herb—to him a balm;
His glance cuts through right to the quick,
Just like an eagle's, sharpened keen.

21

The old one lifts his arm with effort,
Exactly like a crooked branch:
—The German must have lost his way here,
A captive, he crawls around here still.

18.

ער פּאַסט זיך דאָ אַזוי אַרײַן
צווישן די מעכטיקע געוויקסן;
פֿון די דערמאָנונגען ער מאַכט מיך פֿרײַ
און קערט מיר טייקעף אום צוריק זיי.

פֿאַרוווּנדערט קוק איך שטיל אַף אים,
ווי אַף דער אומבאַגרײַפֿטער שיינהייט;
עס איז מיר אָנגענעם זײַן שטים,
האַגאַם זײַן לאָשן איך פֿאַרשטיי ניט.

19.

אַ יעדער באַרג איז אים אַ הויז
און אַ געצעלט אים יעדער בוים איז;
אין זײַנע קנייטשן כ׳לייען אויס
די האַרבקייט פֿון אָט די מעקוימעס.

קיין צוטריט ניט צו זײַן געזונט,
זײַן מאַכט איבער דער צײַט פֿאַרשפּרייט זיך;
ער שלאָגט זיך דאָ אי מיט דער זון,
אי מיט דער באַרגיקער פֿאַרפּלייצונג.

20.

ער שלאָגט זיך קלוג. ער קומט זיי בײַ,
דערנאָכדעם ווערן זיי שוין פֿרײַנט אים;
און, ווי אַ רעגן ס׳גייט פֿאַרבײַ,
און פֿונדאָסנײַ — אַן אויפֿגעשײַנטער.

ס׳איז יעדער טײַך אים צו דער האַנט
און אים אַ זאַלב — איז יעדער קרײַטער;
זײַן בליק שנײַדט דורך זיך ביז צום ראַנד,
ווי בא אַן אָדלער, שאַרף געלײַטערט.

21.

די האַנט הייבט אויף דער זאָקן שווער,
פּונקט ווי אַ צווײַג אַן אויסגעקרומטער:
— דער דײַטש איז ניט דערגאַן אַהער, —
געפֿאַנגען קריכט ער שטיל אַרום דאָ.

Thrice more solemn are the heights
And thrice more regal is the stillness,
Since the German greed that once came here
Crawling on its belly—was destroyed.

22

In a dark corroded cave,
Worn down by wind and parched by sun, —
There lies, once borne here by a snowdrift,
An old rust-eaten German helmet.

A lizard crawls around inside it,
A hidden snake quietly observes it;
Once the beer was foaming in it,
Beer of the Reich, the very best Pilsner.

23

No crow's screech ever reaches there,
No flapping of the wings of birds, —
It lies rust-covered, in the cave,
Where the pride of Germany once crawled in.

—Well, German helmet, tell us how
You came here to be a lord and master, —
It turns out, the cave will be your portion,
With its nettles for condiments.

24

Tell it to the indifferent wind,
How the regiments came down the mountain
Fleeing fast and with commotion,
Taking their machine guns and their wagons.

The helmet lies there without a head,
The helmet lies there without a swastika;
From up above, the snore rolls down,
The snore of sleeping mountain-ness.

ס׳איז דרײַ מאָל פֿײַערלעך די הויך
און דרײַ מאָל מאָלכעסדיק די שטילקייט,
וואָס צוגעקראָכן אָפֿן בויך
איז דײַטשלאַנדס גיר אהער — פֿאַרטיליקט.

.22

אין אַ צעפּרעסן-שוואַרצער הייל,
דורך ווינט צעקראַצט, דורך זון צעטראַסקעט, —
פֿאַרטראָגן ליגט פֿון אַ זאָווייִ
אַ דײַטשע זשאַווערדיקע קאַסקע.

אַ יאַשטשערקע קריכט דורך אין איר,
אַ שלאַנג באַטראַכט פֿאַרטײַעט-שטיל זי;
אין איר געשווימיקט האָט דאָס ביר,
דאָס ביר פֿון רײַך, פֿון סאַמע פּילזן.

.23

ס׳הערט פֿון אַ קראָ זיך קיין געשריי,
פֿון פֿליגל הערט זיך קיין געפּאָכע, —
זי ליגט פֿאַרזשאַווערט אין דער הייל,
ווו ס׳איז גערמאַניעס רום פֿאַרקראָכן.

— נו, קאַסקע דײַטשישע, דערצייל,
ווי ביסט געגאַנגען האר און ווירט זײַן, —
ס׳ועט, ווײַזט אויס, סטײַען דיר די הייל
מיט די פּאָר קראָפּעווע-געווירצן.

.24

דערצייל דעם ווייכנדיקן ווינט,
ווי באַרג אַראָפּ זײַנען די פֿאָלקן
געפֿלויגן ראַשיק און געשווינד
מיט קוילנוואָרפֿערס און דוווקאַלקעס.

זי ליגט, די קאַסקע, אָן אַ קאָפּ,
זי ליגט, די קאַסקע, אָן דעם האָקן;
פֿון דר׳הויך דערקײַקלט זיך דער כראָפּ,
דער כראָפּ פֿון שלאָפֿנדיקער באַרג-קייט.

25

A prisoner crawls slowly by,
Holding a swallow. It writhes and squirms:
—His world, was it as cursed for him,
As for that little wriggling bird?

Did he not hold the world by its throat,
As he now holds the little swallow?
Under the cap no trace is seen
Of his filthy yellow hanks of hair.

26

He drags himself, bearing his burden,
Covered with a stolen shawl:
—The mountains, should they not belong
To him together with the caves?

Gritting his teeth, he chokes the bird
And for a while he lingers there:
—Had not someone on the ground below
Told him to bring along some stones?

27

—Burdened he drags himself along,
Despised for shouldering that load:
—Was it then so great the deal
That for a Pilsner beer he made?

His great shame, it never leaves him:
—How long will you be the mountains' guest?
—Look down, German, from the cave.—
From the cave the helmet calls to him.

28

For the third time it's holiday in the mountains
And there's still shooting in the ravines,
But these places were not dishonored
By the echo of the German boots.

.25

ס׳קריכט אַ געפאַנגענער אַדורך,
ער האַלט אַ שוואַלב. ער שוימט און צאַפּלט:
— האָט ניט די וועלט באַ אים, פאַרפּלוכט,
ווי אַט דאָס פייגעלע געצאַפּלט?

האָט ער שוין פאַרן גאָרגל דען,
ווי אַט די שוואַלב, זי ניט געהאַלטן?
אונטער דעם היטל ניט אַ ברעג
זיַין ברודיקע, זיַין געלע פּאַטלע.

.26

ער קריכט מיט לאַסט געלאָדן שווער
אין אַ געניייוועשער פּאַטשיילע:
— צי דען ניט אים האָבן די בערג
באַדאַרפט געהערן מיט די היילן?

די שוואַלב ער גיט מיט קריץ אַ וואַרג
און פּרוּווט אַ וויַילע בליַיבן שטיין נאָך:
— צי דען איז אים אונטערן באַרג
געווען פאַרזאָגט צו טראָגן שטיינער?

.27

באַלייגט מיט לאַסט ער קריכט פאַרביַי,
פון לאַסט אָף פּלייצע, אַ פאַראַכטער:
— איז וואָס־זשע האָט ער פאַר אַ ביַיט
אָף פילון־ביר זיַינעם געמאַכט דאָ?

עס טרעט פון אים די שאַנד ניט אָפּ:
— אָף לאַנג ביסט אין די בערג אַ גאַסט דאָ?
— גיב, דיַיטש, אין הייל אַ קוק אַראָפּ. —
גיט אים פון הייל אַ רוף אַ קאַסקע...

.28

ס׳איז דריַי מאָל יאַנטעוו אין די בערג
און אין די אָפּגרונטיקע שיסן,
וואָס ס׳האָט די רוימען ניט פאַרשוועכט
דער אָפּהילך פון די דיַיטשע שטיוול.

There's no greater joy or gratitude
Than mine when I recall that feat,
That in my land—beaten to the ground,
In yellow rust rots Germany.

29

From a distance it rolled in,
A Red Army song—in measured tones;
I hear the echo in the mountains
From Stalingrad, and down to Moscow.

For him each meadow holds a blessing,
Every river, every beehive,
For this man, a hundred years of age—
All are wishing peace to passers-by.

30

—Was not each one a beehive too,
Of all my homes, all my dear *shtetls*?
The crooked little roofs and walls,
The quiet alleys, now in ruins?

And like a bee, did each not have—
Midst hills of sorrow in its eyes, —
At least a droplet of the dawn,
Day in, day out, flying around?

31

Did not the tempest there pour out
All its fury upon their heads,
Cut them down and disperse them,
Break them down, and make them orphans?

Did not the combat then inflict
Ills upon them of every kind?
And wasn't it then nine times night
To one imaginary dawn?

כ׳וועל מיט קיין גרעסער גליק און פרייד
און דאַנק דעם גורל ניט דערמאָנען,
וואָס אין מײַן לאַנד — צעקלאַפּטערהייד,
אין געלן זשאַווער פוילט גערמאַניע.

.29

פון ווײַט דערקײַקלט זיך אהער
אַ רויטאַרמייִש ליד — געמאָסטן;
כ׳דערהער דעם אָפּהילך אין די בערג
פון סטאַלינגראַד, פון אונטער מאָסקווע.

מיט בראָכע האַלט אים יעדער לאָז,
און יעדער טײַך, און יעדער בינשטאָק,
דער הונדערטיערעדיקער מאָן —
און רו די דורכגייער זיי ווינטשן.

.30

— איז דען קיין בינשטאָק ניט געווען
מײַן יעדער שטוב, מײַן יעדער שטעטל, —
די קרומע דעכעלעך און ווענט,
די שטילע געסלעך, די געפּלעטע?

איז דען אין יעדער, ווי אַ בין —
מיט בערג פון טרויער אין די אויגן, —
כאָטש נאָך אַ טראָפּעלע באַגין
טאָג־אײַן, טאָג־אויס ארומגעפלויגן?

.31

האָט דער שטורעם ניט אָף זיי
דעם צאָרן זײַנעם אויסגעגאָסן
און זיי פאַרשניטן און צעזייט,
און זיי צעבראָכן, און פאַריאָסעמט?

האָט דען געמיטן זיי די שלאַכט
מיט אומגליקן מיקאָל האָמינים?
איז ניט געווען דען נײַן מאָל נאַכט
אָף איין געדאַכטענעם באַגינען?

32

Oh, my massacred Volhynia,
Oh, my slaughtered dear Podolye, –
Yet the forests still are green
And grain is growing in the valleys.

O, my beheaded thousand years
Of Bessarabia and Poland, –
The dawn still rises on the mountains,
The air above them still is pure.

33

Oh, my massacred Volhynia.
Lulled by misfortune, as by strong brew, –
You have no mountains, only the dawn
To place, like a candle, at your head . . .[19]

Here all is still, and all is bright,
The mountain crests, they bloom with snow;
—Welcoming is your threshold, Caucasus,
To stillness, just as to a tempest.

34

To those sleepy heads of yours,
You, who touch the Milky Way, –
The stairs of stone are calling me
To ascend and then be lost in them . . .

And if I ascend, —then what comes after?
If I should reach the mountain top,
Would someone understand my woe
Besides these heights, so sadly mourning?

35

Here, at the feet of your own mountains,
In their stony *rigor mortis*, –
Brought here to you by disaster,
On the ground I'll sit my *shive*.[20]

19. A candle is placed at the head of a dead person.
20. During the seven days of mourning, *shive*, mourners sit on low benches.

.32

מײַן אויסגעקוילעטע וואָלין,
מײַן אויסגעשאָכטענע פּאָדאָליע, —
עס זײַנען דאָך די וועלדער גרין
און ברויטן וואַקסן דאָך אין טאָלן.

מײַנע געקעפּטע טויזנט יאָר
פֿון בעסאַראַביע און פּוילן, —
ס'גייט אויף אַף בערג נאָך דער קאַיאָר,
אַף בערג ז'דער הימל נאָך אַ הוילער.

.33

מײַן אויסגעקוילעטע וואָלין,
פֿאַרוויגט פֿון אומגליק, ווי פֿון האָפֿן, —
האָסט ניט קיין בערג, כאָטש אַ באַגין
אַף שטעלן זיך, ווי ליכט צוקאָפּנס...

און דאָ איז שטיל, און דאָ איז העל,
די באַרג־שפּיצן מיט שנייען צווייטען;
— ס'איז גאַסטפֿרײַנטלעך, קאַווקאַז, דײַן שוועל
פֿאַר שטילקייט גלײַך, ווי פֿאַר געוויטער.

.34

צו דײַנע שלאָפֿנדיקע קעפּ,
וואָס מיט דעם מילכוועג זיך באַרירן, —
מיר רופֿן שטיינעריקע טרעפּ —
זיך אויפֿהייבן און זיך פֿאַרלירן...

און אויב כ'וועל אויף, — איז וואָס דערנאָך?
אויב כ'וועל דעם באַרגנשפּיץ דערגרייכן,
וועט עמעץ דען דערזען מײַן בראָך
אַ כאָטש די אָוולדיקע הייכן?

.35

צופֿיסנס, דאָ, בײַ דײַנע בערג,
אין זייער שטיינערדיקן גליוווער, —
פֿאַרטראָגן דורך דעם בראָך אַהער,
וועל איך אַף דר'ערד זיך זעצן שיווע.

After a thousand painful years—
Annihilated and erased,
Till the dawn will rise from slumber,
Till the daybreak will waken me . . .

36

But even then, the muted noise
Of the streaming shreds that remain of you,
The ferment of your pain and anguish,
Will never be silenced in my heart,

Neither your splendor, nor your dawn
Will ever lull me to my rest,
When I shall call the thousand years
And bid them come to me in a dream . . .

נאָך טויזנט ווייטאָקדיקע יאָר —
פֿאַרשניטענע און אָפּגעמעקטע,
ביז אויפֿוואַכן וועט דער קאַיאָר,
ביז דער באַגין וועט מיך אַ וועק טאָן...

.36

אָבער אויך דאַן, ווען דער געַרויש
פֿון דײַנע שטראָמיקע געדרויבן
דעם ווײ און צאָרנדיקן ברויז
באַ מיר אין האַרצן ניט פֿאַרטויבן.

און ניט דײַן פּראַכט, און ניט דײַן קאַיאָר
וועט ניט פֿאַרשלעפֿערן מיט רו מיך,
ווען רופֿן כ׳וועל די טויזנט יאָר
צו כאַלעם זאָלן זיי מיר קומען...

THE MUSE

I remember not, before or after,
I fade on the sharp crest of a wave—
But my mother, - is standing beside me,
As was her way. At night. In my childhood.

When she knew not if I were asleep,
When she listened to hear, if I breathed—
She would come to me barefoot—and running,
And from fear—her steps were unsteady.

On that wave—her pale slender hand
With its touch so tender and mild;
Oh, I remember the song's melody
When she sang her children to sleep.

When I cannot recapture her voice,
When her gaze is cast down somewhere else,
Still she rocks me and sings as before
And I—I am swooning with bliss.

Endlessly, winds are pursuing,
Her own song of dawn they assail
But my mother . . . she stands there beside me.
As was her way, at night, in my childhood.

(1948)

די מוזע

איך געדענק ניט, וואָס שפּעטער, וואָס פריִער,
אַף אַ כוואַליע אין כאַלעף פאַרשווינד איך. —
נאָר די מאַמע, — זי שטייט נעבן מיר.
ווי אַמאָל. ווי באַנאַכט. אין דער קינדהייט.

ווען זי האָט ניט געוווּסט צי איך שלאָף.
ווען זי האָט ניט געהערט, צי איך אָטעם —
און איז באָרוועס אַראָפּ און — אַ לאָף,
און פון שרעק ניט געוווּסט — ווי אַ טראָט טאָן.

אַף דער כוואַליע — איר בלאַסלעכע האַנט
מיט אַ צערטלעכן ריר מיט אַ מילדן;
אָ, איך האָב איר ניגן דערמאַנט,
וואָס מיט אים זי פאַרוויגט האָט די קינדער.

אַז איך קאָן ניט דעריאָגן איר קאָל,
אַז אַראָפּגעלאָזט ערגעץ איר בליק איז;
נאָר זי וויגט מיך און זינגט ווי אַמאָל
און איך — איך גיי אויס פון מעסיקעס.

ס'יאָגן ווינטן זיך אָן, אָן אַ שיר.
זיי באַפאַלן דאָס ליד, דאָס באַגינטע;
נאָר די מאַמע... זי שטייט נעבן מיר.
ווי אַמאָל, ווי באַנאַכט אין דער קינדהייט...

.1948

UNISON

It's not so hard for a twig to bend down gently
To welcome as a guest the nightingale;
And become intoxicated with its honey,
And not be mindful of the pain it feels.

Kindred—it seems—the song might make those two.
The tree itself sings out from the nightingale . . .
Perhaps that creature's dazzling song is born,
Because the juices of the two are trickling through it . . .

A little bending is no hardship for the twig.
Like bearing fruit—the pain itself is sweet;
—Then what is left for the twig, when the fruit has fallen,
Or when the nightingale has flown away?

(1948)

באַהעפטונג

ניט שווער דעם צווײַגעלע איז שטיל זיך אָנבויגן
און מאַכנים־אוירעך זײַן דעם סאָלאָווײ;
און זיך פאַרשיקערן מיט זײַנע האָניקן,
און ניט דערמאָנען זיך, אז ס׳טוט דעם ווײ.

עס דוכט: — אָן אייגענע — עס קער דעם ליד זיך אָן.
דער בוים זינגט אויך זיך אוים פון סאָלאָווײ...
געבוירן ווערט עפשער דאָס ליד דאָס בליציקע,
ווײַל ס׳ריזלען זאַפטן שוין אין דעם פון צווײ...

קיין לאַסט דעם צווײַגל איז דער נויג דער קורצינקער.
ווי פון באַפרוכפערונג — דער זיסער ווײ;
— וואָס בלײַבט דעם צווײַגל דען, ווען ס׳רײַסט די
פרוכט זיך אָפּ,
ווען ס׳פליט אַוועק צוריק דער סאָלאָווײ?

.1948

AUTUMN

The yellow stains no longer hurt the grass.
The leaves no longer rustle. Curled up together, —they sleep.
And from that sleep a leaf sets out upon the road,
Just like a little golden mouse, that could not find its nest.

The market is not guarded. Whoever wants may enter:
The wind. The cold. The whipping rain.
And—nobody's there. Only the gloom itself,
Though a buzz comes floating by, and expires in passing.

On foot a bee is hurrying across the uncombed sand.
Its belly is ringed with heavy hoops of gold:
It plows the earth as it goes, and never dallies.—
Suddenly, it springs head over heels—as if right out of a fire.

Then it lifts its little wings—lopsided.
As if it wished to drag the whole dismal world under a small broken parasol,
And topples over. It falls with such a feeble dying buzz:
—The stillness is already heading toward the park for autumn . . .

(1948)

האַרבסט

די געלע פֿליאַמעס טוען שוין ניט ווי דעם גראָז.
די בלעטער שאָרכען שוין ניט מער. צונויפֿגעדרייט, — זיי שלאָפֿן.
און פֿונעם שלאָף גיט איינע זיך איבערן וועג אַ לאָז,
פֿונקט ווי אַ גאָלדן מײַזעלע, וואָס האָט איר נאָרע ניט געטראָפֿן.

דער מאַרק איז ניט באַוואַכט. ס'קאָן ווער סע וויל אַרײַן:
דער ווינט. די קעלט. דער שמײַסנדיקער רעגן
און — קיינער ניט. דער אומעט בלויז אַליין זאָל זײַן,
נאָר ס'פֿליסטערט דורך אַ זשום, פֿאַרגייט זיך אונטערוועגנס.

אַ בין זיך אײַלט צופֿוס איבער דעם ניט פֿאַרקעמטן זאַמד.
איר בויך געשמידט אין שווערע גין־גאָלדענע רייפֿן:
די ערד זי אַקערט גייענדיק, אינערגעץ ניט געזאַמט. —
זי גיט אַ שטעל זיך אַפֿן קאָפּ און — גלײַך, ווי פֿון אַ סרייפֿע.

אָט גיט זי נאָך די פֿליגעלעך אַ הייב — צעקרומט.
ווי אונטער אַ צעבראָכן זאָנטיקל די וועלט זי שלעפּט אַף
זיך די טריבע
און קערט זיך איבער. פֿאַלט מיט אַזאַ דינעם גויסעסדיקן זשום:
— די שטילקייט קלײַבט זיך שוין אין פֿאַרק אַף האַרבסט אַריבער...

.1948

THE DEWS

On thin naked branches, by the wind possessed,
Invisibly the dews at dawn are sprouting.
Like little earrings, woven of light and flame—
Descending from the sun on fine-spun threads.

The dawn—that polisher of diamonds—never tires,
Of weaving and unweaving the tangled branches;
And the sky is young, and the sky is clear,
And the earth is golden, calm, and good.

Oh, look, here it comes—all festooned in dew.
As if descending from the sky with dazzling luster
A sea of tiny lamps, both big and small,
That catch each ray—amazed and merry.

Sometimes there came another, —like a crystal vase,
In which were poured up to the very brim
Countless little flames of frosty blue—
And studded everywhere with crumbled diamonds.

It seems: —should one but breathe on it so slightly,
A song would flow from it, so crystal pure, —
And where the little leaves once windlike rushed,
Now diamonds play—polished by the dawn.

(1948)

טויען

אַף צווײַגלעך נאַקעטע, באַנומענע פֿון ווינט,
שפּראָצן זיך אומזיכטיק פֿאַנאַנדער טויען אין באַגינען.
ווי אוירינגלעך פֿון שײַן און פֿלאַם געשפּינט —
אַראָפּגעלאָזטע פֿון דער זון אַף פֿעדימלעך אַף דינע.

עס ווערט דער בריליאַנטן־שלייפֿער — דער קאַיאָר
ניט מיד אַף צווײַג־געוועב זיי אײַנוועבן און טײלען;
און ס׳איז דער הימל יונג, און ס׳איז דער הימל קלאָר.
און ס׳איז די ערד אַ גאָלדענע, אַ גוטע און אַ שטילע.

דאָ זעט אָ קומט — באַפּוצט מיט טויען אויס.
ווי פֿונעם הימל אַן אַראָפּגעלאָזטע בלענדנדיקע ליוסטרע
מיט לעמפּעלעך אַ יאַם פֿון קליין און גרויס.
וואָס כאַפּן יעדן שטראַל — פֿאַרגאַפֿט און לוסטיק.

דאָרט פֿלעגט אַ צווייטער, ווי אַ וואַזע פֿון קרישטאָל,
אַן אָנגעגאָסענע ביז צו די סאַמע ראַנדן
מיט בלויע פֿראָסטן פֿלעמלעך אָן אַ צאָל,
באַזעצט אַרום מיט אָנגעברעקלטע בריליאַנטן.

עס דוכט: — אַ ריר פֿון ווײַט זיי מיטן אָטעם בלויז,
וועט אַ קרישטאָל־געזאַנג צעגיין זיך אַזאַ דינער, —
און דאָרט, ווו בלעטלעך האָבן ווינטלדיק גערוישט
שפּילן בריליאַנטן איצט — געשלייפֿטע פֿון באַגינען.

.1948

HALF THE WORLD IN SHADOW

The sun tries out its gold first on the clouds,
To see if through and through it clings to them.
And if they have quite properly been painted,
They look like the rosy hide of some young chamois.

Next it heads for the mountains, already waiting from before.
They're sitting there like huge fermenting *khales;*[21]
As if with yolk, the sun brushes them so lightly,
Then lowers itself down—wherever there's a cottage or a stable.

It's no longer early. The blacksmith's hammer is ringing out.
The mountains' rims are soon saddled by the clouds;
Then solemnly the sun usurps the center,
And yet full half a world still lies in shadow . . .

(1948)

21. A *khale* is a woven white bread, baked especially for the Sabbath. It is smeared with yolk to make it shiny.

אַ האַלבע וועלט אין שאָטן

אַף וואָלקנס פּרוּווט צוערשט די זון איר גאָלד.
צי גיט עס דורכדרינגלעך און פּעסט אַף זיי אַ נעם זיך.
און ווען זיי זײַנען ווי געהעריק שוין באַמאָלט
און זעען אויס, ווי ראָזע פּעל פון יונגע געמזעס.

דאָן גייט זי איבער צו די בערג, וואָס וואַרטן נאָך פון פריִער.
וואָס זיצן, ווי די הויכע אויפגעיווירטע כּאַלעס;
זי גיט, ווי מיט אַ גערלכל אַלע זיי אַ לײַכטן שמיד
און לאָזט זיך נידערן — ווּ נאָר אַ שטיבל און אַ שטאַל איז.

ס'איז שוין ניט פרי. עס הערט זיך שוין דער קלונג פון שמיד.
די קאָנטורן פון בערג זײַנען מיט וואָלקנס שוין געזאָטלט;
די זון פאַרכאַפּט שוין פײַערלעך די מיט,
נאָר ס'ליגט נאָך אַלץ אַ האַלבע וועלט אין שאָטן...

.1948

A WOMAN WITH A CHILD

In the morning there's a woman with a child in the mountains.
Like a Madonna, she carries it close in her arms;
—Thank you, silent dawn, still hidden in mist,
For not also hiding from me this human splendor:

In the morning there's a woman with a child in the mountains.
Along the way, a quiet willow tree briefly detains them:
The divide between sky and mountain is still green,
Just a quick glance—and it reminds me of Galilee . . .

In the morning there's a woman with a child in mountains,
Her head is turned sideways on her two narrow shoulders:
A light scarf is fluttering, enchanted by the wind, —
But one sees there no donkey, nor is there a manger . . .

In the morning there's a woman with a child in mountains.
A glow overtakes them, like a rainbow after rain;
She walks not, she floats. Then she vanishes in the glow.
It's good, that no teardrop weighs down her eyes.

She goes quickly, liltingly, just like a wave,
One of a gentle and billowy kind . . .
No, not a Madonna carrying her child,
—Just a Cossack woman, simply a mother;

Her husband is a Cossack – maybe even a Jew.
And possibly—a peasant. Or possibly—a soldier;
I pass by her daily and her footsteps I bless:
—How good, that the world has already borne its Galilee . . .

(1948)

אַ פרוי מיט אַ קינד

אַ פרוי אינדערפרי אין די בערג מיט אַ קינד.
זי טראָגט אַף די הענט עס, אַט ווי אַ מאַדאָנע;
— אַ דאַנק דיר, פאַרנעבלטער, שטילער באַגין,
די מענטשלעכע פּראַכט אויך באַהאַלטסט פאַר מיר דאָ ניט:

אַ פרוי אינדערפרי אין די בערג מיט אַ קינד,
אַ ווערבע טוט שטיל זיי אין וועג אַ פאַרהאַלט:
דער פּאַס צווישן בערג און דעם הימל נאָך גרינט.
אַן אויגנבליק נאָך — און כ'דערמאָן זיך אין גאַליל...

אַ פרוי אינדערפרי אין די בערג מיט אַ קינד,
דער קאָפּ אין דער זײַט צו די אַקסל די שמאָלע:
אַ שאַלעכל פלאַטערט, פאַרקישעפט פון ווינט, —
מע זעט ניט קיין אייזל, מע זעט ניט קיין זשאָלעב...

אַ פרוי אינדערפרי אין די בערג מיט אַ קינד.
די שײַן איבער זיי, ווי פון רעגן און בויגן;
זי גייט ניט, זי שוועבט. אין דער שײַן זי פאַרשווינדט,
ס'איז גוט, וואָס קיין טרער מאַכט ניט שווער אירע אויגן.

זי גייט אַזוי זינגענדיק-שנעל, ווי אַן אינד.
אַ לײַכטע אַזאַ מין, אַ צאַרטע אַזאַ מין...
ניין, ניט קיין מאַדאָנע זיך טראָגט מיטן קינד.
— אַ יונגע קאַזאַטשקע, אַ פּאַשעטע מאַמע;

איר מאַן איז אַ קאַזאַק און עפּשער — אַ ייִד.
און, מעגלעך — אַ פּויער. און, מעגלעך — אַ טשאַליער;
כ'באַגלייט זי אין טאָג און איך בענטש אירע טריט:
— ווי גוט, וואָס די וועלט האָט שוין אָפּגעהאַט גאַליל...

.1948

AN ECHO

Summers of mine have passed here long ago,
Like flying storks that disappear into the clouds;
It seems to me: —I hear their voices calling—
Perhaps in the wind, or in the surging waves.

—Should I whistle to them, as in my carefree youth?
—There, with a clap of hands, a loud hoot goes flying towards them.
All vanished now. This summer too already waits in line
All set for flight, just like a stork . . .

Either from the sounding sea, or from the silent mountains,
Or from the applause that comes from my own two palms, —
A seven-fold echo then makes itself heard,
It's mine. It is not lost. I recognize it.

Anyone would recognize it. It multiplies unceasingly,
As ripples in water from a stone, from wind and surf;
Here have my summers passed so long ago,
Like flying storks that disappear into the clouds . . .

(1948)

ווידערקאָל

דאָ זײַנען זומערס מײַנע דורכגעגאַן אַמאָל,
ווי אין וואָלקנס גייען דורך פֿאַרשווינדנדיקע בושלען ;
מיר דוכט : — איך הער דאָ זייער קאָל —
צי אינעם ווינט, צי אינעם כוואַליעדיקן צושלאָג.

— אַ פֿײַף געבן צו זיי פֿאַרשײַט, ווי יונגערהייט ?
— אָט פֿליט מיט פֿליעסק צו זיי אַ הילכיקער אאו־ו שוין.
פֿאַרשווונדענע. אויך אָט אַ דער אָ זומער איז אין ריי
שוין גרייט צום אָפּפֿלי, ווי אַ בושל...

צי פֿונעם רוישנדיקן יאַם, צי פֿון די שווײַגנדיקע בערג,
צי אָף דעם פֿליעסקענדיקן קלאַנג פֿון מײַנע דלאָניעס, —
אַ ווידערקאָל אַ זיבנפֿאַכיקס זיך דערהערט,
ס׳איז מײַנס. ס׳איז ניט פֿאַרלוירן. איך דערקאָן עס.

דערקאָנען וועט עס יעדערער. סע מערט זיך אָן אַ צאָל.
ווי וואַסערקרײַזן פֿון אַ שטיין פֿון ווינט און צושלאָג ;
דאָ זײַנען מײַנע זומערס שוין אַדורכגעגאַן אַמאָל,
ווי אין די וואָלקנס גייען דורב פֿאַרשווינדנדיקע בושלען...

.1948

AN EVENING STROLL

On an evening stroll, amid the noises of the street,
A butterfly flies toward me, lands upon my heart;
—From where comes such a pleasant, such a welcome guest?
—And why so late? See, the night's already falling . . .

The darkness all around us spreads its borders
And the stars light up one another and then fall;
Only I with my welcome guest—beside me
Go strolling in the street, as with a bride.

A trolley, passing by, waves to us a hurrah,
An omnibus sends us – a rain of fireworks.
—Where do you order me to go, my guest, for this short while?
—Perhaps, my guest, you'll rest just for a moment?

As if spellbound, we two continue strolling,
But we don't let ourselves be lulled to sleep—
Then with the slightest buzz, as if through tissue paper,
My guest - ready to take flight, spreads out its wings

And through their transparency shows me: —what's beyond,
Where the heavens are melting – golden-hued, and clear,
For all the summer songbirds are already there,
Only you, my guest, are missing from the choir.

(1948)

אָוונט־שפּאַציר

אַפן פאַרנאַכטיקן שפּאַציר, אין טומל פון דער גאַס,
פאַרפליט צו מיר אַ שמעטערל, פאַלט צו צום האַרצן;
— פונוואַנען אַזאַ ליבער, אַזאַ אָנגעלייגטער גאַסט?
— וואָס אַזוי שפּעט? עס פאַלט דאָך שוין די נאַכט צו...

אַ טונקלקייט צעשפרייט דאָך שוין דער ראַנד
און שטערן צינדן איינס באַם צווייטן זיך און פאַלן;
נאָר מיט מײַן אָנגעלייגטן גאַסט — באַנאַנד
שפּאַצירן לאָז איך זיך אין גאַס, ווי מיט אַ קאַלע.

אָט מאַכט פאַר אונדז אַ וויווע דער טראַמוויַי,
אָט לאָזט אונדז דער טראָליבוס — פײַערווערק אַ רעגן;
— וווּהין באַפעלסטו מיר, מײַן גאַסט, אַף אָט דער ווײַל?
— וועסט עפשער אָפרוען, מײַן גאַסט, אַ רעגע?

ווי אין קישעף דויערט דער שפּאַציר,
נאָר פונעם קישעף זיך ניט לאָזנדיק פאַרוויגן, —
גיט מיט אַ דינעם זשום, ווי דורך פאַפראָס־פאַפיר
מײַן גאַסט — צום אָפפלי אַ צעלאָז די פליגל

און ווײַזט מיר דורכזיכטיק מיט זיי: — צום ראַנד,
וווּ ס'טריפן הימלען — גאָלדענע און העלע,
שוין אַלע זינג־פייגל דעם זומערס דאָרט פאַראַן,
נאָר דו אַליין פעלסט אויס אין דער קאַפעלע.

.1948

THE ORCHESTRA

Without even a wink, —just to the ear—
As if it were prearranged, as if predestined, —
A little spring, once lost among mountains,
Sends out a distant bell-like wake-up call.

—Who comes in next—so delicately ringing,
So its golden sound not fail to join the din?
The dawn gives a flutter, like a wind-blown tuft of hair, upon the spring,
And then the whole noisy orchestra joyfully chimes in—

In unison. At once. Like a sudden downpour.
Clanging and scraping. Squeaks and drum-beats;
The locust for the lilac makes a dash,
And pipers roll over laughing on their flutes—

At first—hesitantly, they test their throats,
As if their instruments were not quite in tune;
Then the anvil beaters begin to ply with diligence their craft.
And amazed, the cicadas begin to crash their cymbals.

They drown out every clang and every buzz,
Move heaven and earth—and deafen all the neighbors;
When suddenly a bee circles a blossom,
Lifts up its little belly, flutters its tiny wings.

Let it not be confused with the unfolding miracle,
For its chatter can't keep up with all the noise;
While somewhere a little fly wriggles in a spider's vise,
And joining in, the tree tops sing with awe, just like an organ.

And the *bal-t'file*[22]—on the side. Clad in a green dress coat,
Its forelegs - bent, as if it were confessing—
Yet not unnoticed, breaks off its silent praying,
And with its legs saws off the head of a singing cicada.

22. *bal-t'file*: In the synagogue, the person who leads the congregation in communal prayer.

די קאַפּעלע

אַפּילע ניט קיין ווונק, — אַזוי, אַפֿן געהער —
ווי אָפּגערעדט פֿאַרפֿריר, אַזוי לויט די באַרופֿן, —
הייבט אָן אַ קוועלכל, אַ פֿאַרלוירנס אין די בערג
מיט אַזאַ ווייַטן גלעקלדיקן אופֿוואַך.

— ווער גייט דער צווייטער — קלינגענדיק און דין,
דער קלאַנג פֿון גאָלד זאָל אין דעם רויש ניט פֿעלן?
ס׳גיט אַפֿן קוועלכל, ווי אַ טשוב אַ פּלאַטער, דער באַגין
און ראַשיק קוועלט אַרייַן די גאַנצענע קאַפּעלע —

איניינעם. מיט אַמאָל. גלייַך ווי אַ רעגנדיקער גאָס
פֿון קלאַנג און קריץ. פֿון סקריפּ און פֿון געפּייַקל;
אָט גיט זיך אָף די בעז דער איישעריק אַ לאָז
און ס׳גיבן פּייַפֿערס אָף די פֿלייטעס זיך אַ קייַקל —

צוערשט — נאָך אומזיכער. די גאָרגלען נאָר אַ פּרווו,
ווי עפּעס ניט מיט אַלץ אין די קליי־זעמער גלאַט איז;
נאָר שמידערס טוען שוין מיט פֿלייַס זייער באַרוף
און ס׳צימבלען שוין פֿאַרגאַפֿט אָף צימבלען די ציקאַדעס.

זיי שטייַגן איבער יעדן קלאַנג און זשום,
זיי רייַסן אייַן די וועלט — פֿאַרטויבן יעדן שאָכן;
עס גיט אַ דריי אַ בין זיך אָף דער בלום,
זי הייבט דאָס בייַכל אויף, מיט פֿליגעלעך אַ פֿאָכע,

מע זאָל זי ניט מעוואַלאַוול זייַן בעשאַס דעם נעם,
זי קאָן מיט איר געבלעבל נאָך דעם ראַש ניט נאָכגיין;
און ערגעץ צאַפּלט שוין אַ פֿליגעלע באַם שפּין אין קלעם
און שפּיצןביימער זינגען צו מיט פֿאָרכט, ווי אָף אָן אָרגל.

און דער „באַל־טפֿילע״ — אין אַ זייַט. פֿאַרפּוצט אין
גרינעם פֿראַק,
די פֿאָדער־פֿיס — אין בראָך, ווי זייַן ער וואָלט זיך
דאָרט מיסוואַדע, —
ניט אומבאַמערקט מיט זיי בעלאָכאָש אַ פֿאַרהאַק,
זעגט אָפּ מיט זיי דעם קאָפּ באַ אַ צעזונגענער ציקאַדע.

But the joy of living is not interrupted,
Nor may even one of the thousand sounds be absent, —
And over this early morning chorale
Presides this wondrous golden orchestra.

נאָר ס׳רײַסט ניט איבער זיך די פרייד פון זײַן,
קיין איינער פון די טויזנט קלאַנגען טאָר ניט פעלן, —
און פאַרגעזעצט עס ווערט ס׳פרימאָרגיקע געזאַנג
פון דער פאַרגאַפטער גאָלדענער קאַפּעלע.

WORRY

It's enough for a ray of sun to tickle a blossom,
For the wind to grab by a tuft of leaves a shrub, —
The smith-worm[23] folds up its wings like an apron, —ready,
And God alone knows how it could obtain an anvil.

Its stiffened whiskers bristle menacingly,
The impatient green things get tangled in its legs;
—A waste of time, one should only forge when the iron's hot,-
The creeping little ants he so informs.

A sudden flight, a jumping, a sense of threat—
From blade to blade of grass, blossom to blossom;
One—it lets go, a second it pursues:
—Pray, does anyone need soldering or forging?

Its beckoning hammer is itself then melted down
Into a thousand, bell-like fleeing worries—
And the smith-worm quite forgets his craft of smithing
Until the sunrise of the coming morning.

23. smith-worm: One of a family of cicada-like insects.

זאָרג

גענוג, אַז ס'זאָל אַ שטראַל אַ קיצל טאָן אַ קווייט,
אַז אָנכאַפּן דער ווינט אַ קוסט זאָל פֿאַר דער פּאַטלע, —
פֿאַרשטעקט דער שמיד־וואָרעם די פֿליגל, ווי אַ פֿאַרטעך, — גרייט.
און ס'ווייסט איין גאָט, ווי ער באַשטעלט זיך אַ קאָוואַדלע.

די האַרטע וואָנצעם זײַנע רודערן זיך בייז,
מיט גרינעם אומגעדולד זיי פּלאָנטען אין די פּים זיך;
— אַ שאָד די צײַט, און שמידן דאַרף מען ווען ס'איז הײם, —
לאָזט ער די קריכנדיקע מורעשקעס צו וויסן.

ס'איז אַ געפּלי, אַ שפּרונגערײַ און אַ געפּאַר
פֿון גראָז צו גראָז, פֿון קווייטעלע צו קייטל;
איינעם — אַדורכגעלאָזט, דעם צווייטן יאָגט ער נאָך:
— דאַרף עפּשער עמעץ וואָס פֿאַרקאָווען, צי פֿאַרלייטן?

אַליין זיך שמעלצט זײַן רופֿנדיקער האַמער אײַן
אין טויזנט־גלעקלדיקע פֿליִענדיקע זאָרגן —
און עס פֿאַרגעסט דער שמיד־וואָרעם זײַן שמידערײַ
ביז צו דעם זון־אויפֿגאַנג פֿון קומענדן פֿרימאָרגן.

SELF-OBLIVION

Why then should not a man give up his bounty,
When every living thing gives of itself with bliss. —
When the sun falls to the sea, and the stalk falls to the thresher, —
Why then should not a man depart with song,
When at night, the cricket does not tire of chirping,
When by day, the smith-worm does not cease his hammering,
And the cicada plays its cymbals till it's near to bursting,
And the wind beats leaf on leaf, like cymbals one on one,
And blades of grass curling up resound so loudly,
And each one plays upon itself, as on a flute,
As if each one had need of pouring itself out—
And who of this fine orchestra is falling off its feet,
And one among them—has already lost its place, —
And though the cuckoo bird is nowhere to be found,
It seems as if it cuckoos all day long,
And though there are no nightingales around,
The mountain spring gives way to fits of trilling, —
Each one competes, and each one tries its best,
And each one strives to outdo all the others,
As if each felt the need to fill to brimming
The entire world with sound, the entire world with gold.
And already it is full, already overflowing,
With innumerable pourings, and still more to come,
And lulled to sleep, the dozing sea lies still
And seems to moan in its sleep, while dreaming of the joy
In each incomprehensible and stirring voice,
Deeper yet than the sea, and wider flooding, —
Why then should not a man give up his bounty,
When every living thing gives of itself with bliss.

זעלבסטפאַרגעסונג

איז ווי־זשע זאָל דער מענטש ניט אָפּגעבן זײַן גאָב,
ווי יעטווידער באַל־כײַ מיט כעדווע גיט זיך אָפּ. —
ווען ס׳פאַלט די זון צום יאַם, ווי ס׳פאַלט צום דראָש אַ זאַנג, —
איז ווי־זשע זאָל דער מענטש ניט אָפּגיין מיט געזאַנג,
אַז ס׳ווערט אַ נאַכט די גריל פון דרעליעווען ניט מיד,
און ס׳הערט אַ טאָג ניט אויף צו האַמערן דער שמיד,
און די ציקאַדע צימבלט, שיר ניט וואָס זי פלאַצט
און ווינט מיט בלאַט אַן בלאַט, גלײַך ווי מיט טאַץ און טאַץ,
און גראָזן גרײַזלען אוים זיך הילכיק, אַף אַ קאָל,
און יעדע שפילט אַף זיך, ווי אַף אַ פײַפיאָל,
ווי אָנגיסן באַדאַרפט אַ יעדער איינער וואָלט
און ווער פון דער קאַפּעלע — פון די פים שוין פאַלט,
און עמעצער פון איר — שוין ווייסט ניט ווו ער האַלט, —
און כאָטש קיין קוקו איז אינערגעץ דאָ ניטאָ,
איז דאַכט זיך, אַז זי קוקעט אויך אַ גאַנצן טאָג,
און כאָטש ס׳איז ניט פאַראַנען דאַ קיין נאַכטיגאַל,
פאַרגייט מיט טרעלן זיך דער באַרגנקוואַל, —
און יעדערער פאַרלויפט, און יעדערער זיך פלײַסט,
און איבערשטײַגן איינס דעם אַנדערן זיך רײַסט,
ווי אָנגיסן באַדאַרפט אַ יעדער איינער וואָלט
די גאַנצע וועלט מיט קלאַנג, די גאַנצע וועלט מיט גאָלד,
און אָט איז זי שוין פול, ס׳גייט איבער שוין דער ראַנד,
און ס׳גיסט זיך אָן אַ צאָל, און נאָך, ווידעראַנאַנד,
דער דרעמלדיקער יאַם אַן אײַנגעוויגטער ליגט
ער קרעכצט, דאַכט זיך, פון שלאָף און ס׳כאָלעמט זיך אים גליק
פון יעדער אומפאַרשטענדלעכער און וועקנדיקער שטים,
וואָס טיפער איז פון אים, פאַרפלייצנדער פון אים, —
איז ווי־זשע זאָל דער מענטש ניט אָפּגעבן זײַן גאָב,
ווי יעטווידער באַל־כײַ מיט כעדווע גיט זיך אָפּ?

FIGARO

At once the entire orchestra stops playing,
And the radio swings and sways along with its waves, —
A flourish up high, then a roll down low,
And with joy and sorrow—rainbowlike: —*Figaro.*

In the trees—a frolick, amid the leaves—a rustling
And another little droplet he delivers to the dew;
On their little stalks flowers are listening, as if enchanted,
And for him they open up all their doorways and gates.

Such a silvery mountain spring gushes forth from him,
No nightingale could ever pour out such sweetness;
Bewitched, on a mountain a rose bends its head,
And applauds with its petals—*bravo, bravissimo.*

Though nowhere around do we see the nightingale,
Though nowhere do we see it flapping its wings, —
Only the trills—in the dazzle of moon and snow
Ring out like bells—*Figaro, Figaro, Figaro.*

One moment there's laughter, another there's crying
And then both together roll down to his feet, —
And now the whole orchestra itself is applauding:
The butterflies—*bravo.* The birds—*bravissimo.*

The mountains grow taller and still deeper the sea
When heard is the voice of man from its source, —
It's here. It's there. Everywhere—celebration.
—*Bravo, bravissimo,* —*Figaro, Figaro.*

פ י ג אַ ר אָ

מיט אַמאָל שטעלט די גאַנצע קאַפּעלע זיך אָפּ,
ס׳גיט זיך בויגיק די ראַדיאָ אַף די כוואַליעס אַ וויג אַרײַן, —
זיך אַ ציקל אינדר׳הויך און אַ קײַקל אַראָפּ
און מיט טרויער און לוסט — רעגנבויגנדיק: — פיגאַראָ.

אַף די ביימער — אַ שפּיל, צווישן בלעטער — אַ שאָרך
און אַ טריפּ ער דערלאַנגט אין די טראָפּעלעך טוי אַרײַן;
ס׳הערן בלומען אַף שטענגעלעך, ווי אין פאַרשפּראָך
און פאַר אים זיי צעעפענען טירן און טויערן.

אַז אַ זילבערנער באַרגקוואַל פון אים שלאָגט אַרויס,
אַזוי זיס קאָן קיין איין סאָלאָוויי ניט פאַרגיסן זיך;
אַפן באַרג בייגט זיך אָן אַ פאַרצויבערטע רויז
און זי פּאַטשט מיט די בלעטעלעך — בראַוואָ, בראַווּיסימאָ.

אַז מע זעט אים אינערגעץ ניט, דעם סאָלאָוויי,
אַז מע זעט ניט אינערגעץ קיין פּאָך טאָן מיט די פליגל אים, —
נאָר די טרעלן — אין בלענד פון לעוואָנע און שניי
קלינגען גלעקלדיק: — פיגאַראָ, פיגאַראָ, פיגאַראָ.

אָט גיט ער אַ לאָך און אָט גיט ער אַ וויין
און אָט וואַלגערן ביידע באַגלײַך זיך צופיסן אים, —
און עס פּלעסקען די גאַנצע קאַפּעלע אַליין:
די שמעטערלעך — בראַוואָ. די פייגל — בראַווּיסימאָ.

ס׳ווערן העכער די בערג און נאָך טיפער דער יאַם
פון דער מענטשלעכער שטים, פון דעם מענטשלעכן שטאַם, —
זי איז דאָ. זי איז דאָרט. אומעטום — אַ באַזינגערן.
— בראַוואָ, בראַווּיסימאָ. — פיגאַראָ, פיגאַראָ.

SOLO

Whenever all the sounds grow really silent;
When all the nightly orchestra is dozing, —
The hoarsely worrying cricket still is heard,
And its peep grows ever sharper, ever brighter.

It knows no difference if it's night or day,
With the slightest parting rustle it awakens dreams—
Alone it leads them round—to want or wealth,
And waits, no matter which. Time—is no barrier.

It sings its song, when the dream is sweet and pleasant,
The same song, when the dream is hard and bitter, —
And with its thin and silky-rustling murmur
It escorts them back again, just like a loyal guardian.

It knows no difference if it's night or day,
When it works its magic spell, secrets take fright;
What is fancied and what is not—vanish as if on wings
And over all this stillness, it sings out—a solo.

Its meaning—an enigma, a mystery,
Sometimes—it's weak, sometimes—more strident;
From afar a mountain spring chimes in with it,
And a tiny piping voice, that strayed here from somewhere; —

They're trying to reach heaven from the earth,
Stretching out their little throats in song, —
Even though—the peep is only heard in the silence,
It seems—that while asleep, —the whole world hears it . . .

סאָלאָ

ווען ס׳גייען אוים שוין אַלע קלאַנגען שטיל,
ווען ס׳דרעמלט אײַן די גאַנצע נאַכטישע קאַפּעלע, —
הערט זיך נאָך אַלץ די הייזעריק־פֿאַרזאָרגטע גריל
און ס׳ווערט איר פּיפּס געשליפֿענער און העלער.

זי ווייסט ניט קיין האַפּסאָקע צווישן טאָג און נאַכט,
מיט דינסטע שײַדן־שאָרכן וועקט זי די כאַלוימעס —
אַליין זי פֿירט זיי אום — צו אָרעם און צו פּראַכט
און וואַרט, אָן אונטערשייד. די צײַט — קיין צוים איז...

זי זינגט, ווען ס׳איז דער כאָלעם לײַכט און זים,
דאָס נעמלעכע, ווען ס׳איז דער כאָלעם שווער און ביטער, —
און מיט איר דינעם זײַדן־שאָרכיקן געפּלים
באַגלייט זי די כאַלוימעס צוריק, ווי אַ געטרײַער היטער.

זי ווייסט ניט קיין האַפּסאָקע צווישן נאַכט, און טאָג,
אונטער איר צויבער־מי גיבן זיך סוידעס אַ פֿאַרהאָלע;
געדאַכטס און ניט געדאַכטס גיט, ווי אַף פֿליגל אַ פֿאַרטראָג
און איבער גאָר דער שטילקייט זינגט זי — סאָלאָ.

פֿון ניט געשטויגן, ניט געפֿלויגן — דעם באַטײַט,
אַ ווײַלע — שלאָבערדיק, אַ ווײַלע — שטײַפֿער;
עס האַלט אַ באַרגנקוואַל זי אונטער פֿון דער ווײַט,
עפּעס אַ קעלעכל, פֿאַרבלאָנדזשעט פֿון אַ פֿײַפֿער, —

זיי רײַסן זיך צום הימל פֿון דער ערד
מיט אויסגעשטרעקטע זינגענדיקע העלדזער, —
נאָר בלויז — איר פּיפּס זיך אין דער שטילקייט הערט,
עס דוכט — אַ שלאָפֿנדיקע, — הערט די גאַנצע וועלט זי...

THE BAT

It's no longer night, nor yet the day,
The end and the beginning come together;
Suddenly a bat darts swiftly out
In that indefinite in-betweenness,

And glides right through in such a way,
It's like a flying shred of shadow—
Of something, maybe just imagined,
And maybe, everywhere—it's scattered . . .

She hurries home. It's time for her already.
But now she's blinded by the glare
Of the early morning's whiteness,
Melting somewhere on a window.

Wrapping herself in her weekday shawl—
That she pulled up over her head,
Up she flies, down she swoops
In the early morning magic: —

Here just now there was some light,
Then suddenly it's gone again;
And for a while she's lost between
The end of night and the day's beginning.

A swoop—so straight, a swoop—so crooked.
The radiance dies. It's here no more.
And so the bat comes back again
Through that indefinite in-betweenness . . .

(1947)

די פלעדערמויז

ס׳איז שוין ניט נאַכט, ס׳איז נאָך ניט טאָג
דער סאָף און אָנהייב זיך פאַרמישן;
אַ פלעדערמויז גיט זיך אַ טראָג
אין דעם ניט-אָנזעעוודיקן צווישן.

זי גיט זיך אַזאַ גליטש אַדורך,
ווי אַ שטיק פליִענדיקער שאָטן
פון דעם, וואָס עפּשער בלויז זיך דוכט
און, עפּשער, אומעטום — צעשאָטן...

זי אײַלט אַהיים. איר איז שוין צײַט.
נאָר ס׳גיט אָן אָפּשײַן אַ פאַרבלענד זי
פון דער באַגינענדיקער ווײַס,
וואָס שמעלצט זיך ערגעץ אָף אַ פענצטער.

און אין איר וואַכעדיקער שאָל —
איבערן קאָפּ אַרויפגעהויבן,
גיט זי אַ פלי, גיט זי אַ פאַל
אָף דעם באַגינענדיקן צויבער: —

אָט דאָ נאָר וואָס געווען איז ליכט,
נאָר עפּעס זעט מען עס שוין דאָ ניט;
און אָף אַ ווײַלע זי פאַרלירט
דעם סאָף פון נאַכט, פון טאָג דעם אָנהייב.

אַ הוידע — גלײַך, אַ הוידע — קרום.
דער אָפּשײַן שטאַרבט. ער איז ניט הי שוין.
און ס׳קערט די פלעדערמויז זיך אום
דורך דעם ניט-אָנזעעוודיקן צווישן...

.1947

THE RAINBOW

The rain was coming down. Yet that did not disturb it.
With one end it tweaks the heads of mountains,
And with the other it catches the sea as with a bucket,
And weaves upon it a carpet of purest gold.

A gush of foaming blood—it seemed
Upon the trembling plain from either side was spurting;
The rainbow was riding—solemnly and fiercely
Over the clouds, just like a flaming horseman.

The rain was coming down. The rain was shining—
Pierced all through itself by light—a little dawn;
And hiding under it, the rainbow ducked out of sight,
As if behind a rosy, falling curtain.

(1948)

דער רעגנבויגן

דער רעגן איז געגאַן. אים האָט דער רעגן ניט געשטערט.
די בערג פֿאַרטשעפּעט מיט איין עק האָט פֿאַר די קעפּ ער,
מיט צווייטן, ווי אַ קראָמיסלע פֿאַרכאַפּט דעם יאַם האָט ער
און אויסגעשטריקט אַף אים אַ גין־גאָלדענעם טעפּיך.

אַ כלויפּ פֿון בלוט אַ שוימיקער — געדאַכט
האָט אַף דער צאַפּלדיקער פֿלאַך געשפּריצט פֿון ביידע זײַטן;
געריטן האָט דער רעגנבויגן פֿײַערלעך און האַרט
איבער די וואָלקנס, ווי אַ ברענענדיקער רײַטער.

דער רעגן איז געגאַן. דער רעגן האָט געהעלט —
אַליין אַ דורכגעשטאָכענער מיט ליכט — קאַיאָריק;
און אונטער אים האָט זיך דער רעגנבויגן, טײַענדיק, פֿאַרשטעלט,
ווי הינטער אַזאַ ראָזן, פֿאַלנדיקן פֿאָרהאַנג.

.1948

GOOD MORNING

Her dark eyes and a string of pearly teeth, —
The sea carries them here, like a prayer said at dawn;
Nothing more is seen upon the sea—just she alone,
She waits for me at sea with her good morning.

It seems to me—her teeth are winking at me,
With the sharpness of a knife—she bids me follow her;
—Is that a sea gull clapping its wings above us? No, wrong.
It's the ocean's heart beating out its good morning.

Among the pebbles on the beach, her dress is chattering,
And a little worrying breeze is blowing toward the shore;
—Here it comes, her dress. —Suddenly I'm running with the breeze,
—Would I not with my noise sometimes drown out her good morning?

The sun reached out to me a shaft of gold,
So sweet is its caress upon my throat;
I turn, I look around, —as if about to bite,
Her teeth, they give a sudden yank: —good morning.

גוט מאָרגן

די שוואַרצע אויגן און דאָס ווײַסע שנירל ציין, —
עס טראָגט דער יאַם זיי, ווי אַ טפּילע פון קאַיאַר דאָ;
מער זעט מען גאָרניט אַפן יאַם. בלויז — זי אַליין,
זי וואַרט מיך אָפּ אין יאַם מיט איר גוט־מאָרגן.

מיר דוכט — אַ ווונק זי גיט מיר מיט די ציין,
ווי מיט אַ מעסרדיקער שאַרף — איך זאָל איר נאָכגיין;
— פּאַטשט ניט אַ מעווע איבער אונדז? אַ טאָעס. ניין.
עס קלאַפּט דאָס האַרץ פון יאַם מיט איר גוט־מאָרגן.

צווישן די שטײנדלעך אַפן ברעג פלאַפּלט איר קלייד,
עס גייט אַ ווינטעלע צום ברעג מיט זײַנע זאָרגן;
— אָט איז איר קלייד. — גיב איך דאָס ווינטל אַ באַגלייט, —
וועל איך צו מאָל דאָ ניט פאַרפלאַפּלען איר גוט־מאָרגן?

צו מיר האָט אויסגעשטרעקט די זון פון גאָלד אַ שפּיז,
ס'איז אַזוי זיס איר גלעט איבערן גאָרגל;
איך דריי זיך אויס, איך קוק זיך אום, — ווי צו אַ ביס
האָבן זיך ציין אירע אַ צי געטאָן: — אַ גוט־מאָרגן.

ABOUT THE TRANSLATOR

Mary Schulman was born in 1910 in St. Petersburg, Russia, the second of four children. Her father ran a bookbinding business. After enduring the travails of the Russian Revolution, the family returned to the parents' native Latvia, and later emigrated to the United States, the father first, followed by the rest of the family in 1923. A brilliant student, she attended Hunter College in New York City, majoring in mathematics and physics. She taught in the New York City public high schools for many years, meanwhile earning master's degrees from City College in science and mathematics education, and in Russian studies. Always a scholar, in 1963 she published a biographical study of the Zionist philosopher Moses Hess. Upon retiring from teaching, she devoted herself to Jewish studies, first at the YIVO Institute and then at Columbia University, where she earned a doctorate in Slavic and Jewish Studies at the age of seventy-three, becoming the University's oldest recipient of the doctoral degree. Her dissertation topic was Judaic themes in the medieval Slavic Chronicle, for which she learned Polish and Old Church Slavonic. She contributed translations of Holocaust memoirs for the book and documentary, *Lodz Ghetto* (1989). Besides the Markish translation, she was working on several other projects up until her death in 2002 at the age of ninety-two. These include translations of classic Yiddish holiday stories, a comprehensive study of the medieval Jewish traveling merchants of the Silk Routes, and a compilation of historical facts and legends about New York State.

ACKNOWLEDGEMENTS

The Dora Teitelboim Center for Yiddish Culture wishes to acknowledge the support of the National Yiddish Book Center. The Yiddish text was made available through the Steven Spielberg Digital Yiddish Library of the National Yiddish Book Center (www.yiddishbookcenter.org) We also appreciate the patient and studious review of the Yiddish translations by Troim Katz Handler. And thanks to Esther Markish, Peretz's widow and Simon Markish, Peretz's son, for their assistance. Finally, this book could not have been published without the support and encouragement of the members and supporters of the Center. A sheynem dank (Thank you.)

NOTE TO YIDDISH READERS

In order to maintain the authenticity of the original, we have opted to use the original Yiddish text side by side with the English translation. Inherent in using original typefaces is carrying over spelling and punctuation errors from the original. Further, given that the author spent most of his life in the former Soviet Union, Yiddish readers will note that some spelling of words tends not to follow YIVO or Hebrew orthography but instead opts for Soviet spelling. This reflects the time and place in which the poems were written.

THE EDITORS